WHEN HE SAW THE CROWDS - BIBLE STUDIES
UND DA ER DAS VOLK SAH - BIBELSTUDIEN
VOYANT LES FOULES - ÉTUDES BIBLIQUES
AL VER LAS MULTITUDES - ESTUDIOS BÍBLICOS

WHEN HE SAW THE CROWDS - BIBLE STUDIES
UND DA ER DAS VOLK SAH - BIBELSTUDIEN
VOYANT LES FOULES - ÉTUDES BIBLIQUES
AL VER LAS MULTITUDES - ESTUDIOS BÍBLICOS

11th Assembly, World Council of Churches
11. Vollversammlung des Ökumenischen Rates der Kirchen
11e Assemblée du Conseil œcuménique des Églises
11a Asamblea, Consejo Mundial de Iglesias

When He Saw the Crowds - Bible Studies
Und da er das Volk sah - Bibelstudien
Voyant les foules - Études bibliques
Al ver las multitudes - Estudios bíblicos

WCC Publications is the book publishing programme of the World Council of Churches. The WCC is a worldwide fellowship of 352 member churches which represents more than half a billion Christians around the world. The WCC calls its member churches to seek unity, a common public witness and service to others in a world where hope and solidarity are the seeds for justice and peace. The WCC works with people of all faiths seeking reconciliation with the goal of justice, peace, and a more equitable world.
Opinions expressed in WCC Publications are those of the authors.

Production: Lyn van Rooyen, coordinator of WCC Publications
Cover, Book design and typesetting: Juliana Schuch
Printed by: Rudolph Druck - www.ruolphdruck.de
ISBN: 978-2-8254-1816-1

World Council of Churches
150 route de Ferney, P.O. Box 2100
1211 Geneva 2, Switzerland
www.oikoumene.org

CONTENTS

INHALT

TABLE DES MATIÈRES

ÍNDICE

INTRODUCTION

The plenary Bible studies are an important aspect of the work of the assembly. They give participants an opportunity to meet daily around a Bible passage to reflect on the theme and the experience of the assembly. Participants can discern together God's purposes for themselves and the ecumenical movement. They meet in groups which are small enough to allow everyone to contribute and large enough to give a range of perspectives.

The Bible study sessions provide an opportunity for participants to explore the assembly theme together in the light of the biblical texts, knowledge, and experience. To be involved in group Bible study is to be open to one another, to the Bible passage and to the Holy Spirit. It is not to win an argument or to persuade others to a particular point of view. These sessions should be a place where the participants can integrate all they have heard and done in the assembly and discover together the possibilities of transformation that God offers us.

OVERVIEW

Day 2, Thursday, 1 September 2022

Day Theme: *The purpose of God's love in Christ for the whole creation – reconciliation and unity*
Biblical reference: Col 1:19 f. (Eph 1:10) and Mt 9:35 f. (Christ's Compassion)
Plenary Theme: *The purpose of God's love in Christ for the whole creation – reconciliation and unity*
Reflection by: Fr Jack Khalil and Rev. Dr Hyunju Bae

Day 3, Friday, 2 September 2022

Day Theme: *Europe*
Biblical reference: Luke 10:25-37 (Good Samaritan)
Plenary Theme: *Europe*
Reflection by: Prof. Dr Krzysztof Mielcarek

Day 6, Monday, 5 September 2022

Day Theme: *Christ's love – Compassion for life*
Biblical reference: John 9:1-12
Plenary Theme: *Affirming the wholeness of life*
Reflection by: Prof. Dr Diana Tsaghikyan

Day 7, Tuesday, 6 September 2022

Day Theme: *Christ's love – Transforming Discipleship*
Biblical reference: Matthew 15:21-28 (Canaanite woman)
Plenary theme: *Affirming justice and human dignity*
Reflection by: Dr Paulo Ueti

Day 8, Wednesday, 7 September 2022

Day Theme: *Christ's love – The bond of Christian unity and the churches' common witness*
Biblical reference: Matthew 20.20-28
Plenary theme: *Christian Unity and the churches' common witness*
Reflection by: Rev. Dr Kenneth Mtata

Let us pray for one another as we prepare for this task and to participate in the Assembly. Let *Christ's love move the world to reconciliation and unity.*

THE PURPOSE OF GOD'S LOVE IN CHRIST FOR THE WHOLE CREATION—RECONCILIATION AND UNITY

Jack Khalil

[19] *For in him all the fullness of God was pleased to dwell,* [20] *and through him to reconcile to himself all things, whether on earth or in heaven, making peace through the blood of his cross.*

—Colossians 1:19–20

These verses are contained within the Christological hymn in Colossians 1:15–20. Whether this passage comes from a traditional older hymn or is written by St Paul himself in the style of a hymn, it sounds like music to the ear of all those who love God. It associates the divine economy of salvation with the theology of creation by identifying the Redeemer of the world as the Creator who brought everything into existence. The first strophe (vv. 15–18a) reveals the identity of Christ as the creator of all things "in heaven and on earth" (v. 16), concluding with a shift to His being the head of the church (v. 18a). The second strophe (vv. 18b–20) exposes the benefaction of Christ to all creation "whether on earth or in heaven" (v. 20), as evinced by his incarnation (v. 19), passion, death, and resurrection for all humans. It is clearly shown that the historical events, which the second strophe touched upon, are closely related to what the first strophe assures: namely, that Christ is the creator of all things; Christ's love, manifested by reconciling all things to himself through His blood, is rooted in His love shown at the creation of all things. The repetition of the expression "all things . . . in heaven and on earth"—both in the first strophe that talks about their creation and in the second strophe that talks about their reconciliation—validates the previous comment that the reconciliation of all things comes from Christ's love to all things He created. Christ's love is from eternity to eternity. He cares for and guards all things on earth as in heaven, for they are His own.

Christ's love calls us and moves us to reconciliation. It calls us to repent our enmity toward Him (v. 21), which is shown in doing evil toward our neighbour and toward His universe. It is helpful to be aware that our sin toward God is not reduced to blasphemy and ingratitude; rather, it is primarily a humanly relational and ecological sin.

According to Romans 8:7, hostility is a consequence of having a "mind that is set on the flesh," which means striving to please the self and the selfish desires (Gal. 5:16) to the detriment of our co-humans. "Idolatry, sorcery, enmities, strife, jealousy, anger, quarrels, dissensions, factions" (Gal. 5:2) as works of the flesh are some representative examples of relational sins. In this sense, Colossians 1:21 states that enmity from humans toward God exists due to evil deeds.

The fact that sin and evil works turn human beings into enemies of God does not mean that sin brings about mutual enmity between God and humankind, nor that God is hostile to sinners. Such a view is nowhere to be found in the epistles of St Paul. On the contrary, Paul makes it perfectly clear who is hostile to whom when he notes that "the mind that is set on the flesh is hostile to God" (Rom. 8:7) and that enmity exists "in mind because of evil deeds" (Col. 1:21 NAB).

St John Chrysostom notes more precisely: "And what does he entreat? 'Be reconciled unto God.' And he said not, 'Reconcile God to yourselves'; for it is not He that bears enmity, but you; for God never bears enmity."[1] In fact, both the active voice "to reconcile" (καταλλάξαι or ἀποκαταλλάξαι), used in Colossians 1:20 and elsewhere when Paul speaks of God's deed, and the passive voice "to be reconciled" (καταλλάττεσθαι), used when Paul exhorts Christians to be reconciled to God, show beyond doubt that God has reconciled us to Himself.

God reconciles those who became God's enemies, who showed ingratitude to God. And they did so whenever they contributed to conflicts and wars, growing social and economic inequalities, the climate crisis, and the COVID-19 pandemic. The forgiveness of enmity through the death and resurrection of Christ offered peace to all humans who became enemies because of such sinful deeds.

Only the incarnate Son, in whom "all the fullness of God was pleased to dwell" (Col. 1:19), can restore peace where enmity reigns, can reinstitute justice where many still suffer from injustice, can reinstall unity among those who are obscured by "idolatry, sorcery, enmities, strife, jealousy, anger, quarrels, dissensions, factions."

Human beings would never have managed on their own to attain the righteousness necessary for reconciliation with God. With this understanding, the apostle Paul, in verse 20, connects the moment of reconciliation with Christ's death on the Cross ("through the blood of his cross").

The divine blood, shed on the cross for us, by its power to forgive enmity, made peace with all things, "whether on earth or in heaven." In the same way, the salvific death and resurrection of Christ bring unity to all those who are moved by Christ's love. Those who repudiate the selfish love that is the root of sin and learn from Christ's love and unselfish offering will be reconciled through Christ even among themselves. They will respond to Christ's kindness and compassion by embracing love, justice, and peace as tenets of behaviour toward "all things" and all humans, whom Christ loves and for whom He died.

Today we are called together to express gratitude for Christ's love for our world and for all human beings and to reflect in prayer and repentance on our tangible response to his love. We intend with all our hearts to learn from the blood of the cross that we all have to sacrifice and take common action for justice, peace, and reconciliation through Christ, our blessed Lord of Glory.

1. How does Christ's love move us to justice and unity? What do we learn from His love?
2. How can we show gratitude in response to God's love? What are the tangible actions of love toward humans and the whole of the creation that God is moving us to take?

---

1 St. John Chrysostom, "Homilies on Second Corinthians," in New Advent, https://www.newadvent.org/fathers/2202.htm

THE PURPOSE OF GOD'S LOVE IN CHRIST FOR THE WHOLE CREATION—RECONCILIATION AND UNITY

Hyunju Bae

[35] Then Jesus went about all the cities and villages, teaching in their synagogues, and proclaiming the good news of the kingdom, and curing every disease and every sickness. [36] When he saw the crowds, he had compassion for them, because they were harassed and helpless, like sheep without a shepherd. [37] Then he said to his disciples, "The harvest is plentiful, but the labourers are few; [38] therefore ask the Lord of the harvest to send out labourers into his harvest.

—Matthew 9:35–38

Jesus the Compassionate

Matthew 9:35–38 is a crossroads. It looks back on Jesus' ministry, and it also anticipates his teaching on the disciples' mission. Verse 35 summarizes Jesus' actions in Matthew 4:23 by repeating words such as teaching, proclaiming, and curing. These activities are called Jesus' threefold ministry. Jesus enlightened people's minds invited them to open their hearts to the advent of God's reign, and healed their physical illnesses.

Verse 36 reveals that compassion is the driving force behind Jesus' ministry. Jesus had compassion for people who were harassed and helpless. "Harassed" (*eskylmenoi*) originally meant being flayed or skinned. "Helpless" (*errimmenoi*) means to be prostrate or to lie on the ground. People were exploited, dejected, weary, downtrodden, crushed. Jesus responded with compassion to the people, who were like sheep without a shepherd. The Greek verb *splagchnizomai*, which is used in Matthew to describe Jesus' compassion (14:14; 15:32; 18:27; 20:34), derives from the noun *splagchnon*, which means, first, the inner parts of a body or the entrails; second, the heart; and third, love or affection. The compassion that Jesus showed in his acts of mercy (5:7; 9:13) flows spontaneously from the capacity of love to feel and sympathize in the gut, that is, in a holistic way integrating heart and body. Compassion is the ultimate originator of Jesus' threefold ministry.

In 9:37, Jesus discloses his sense of reality in recognizing the imbalance between plentiful harvest and few labourers. This does not lead to despair but to the awareness of the great opportunity and to prayer; in the following verse, Jesus exhorts his disciples to pray that the Lord of the harvest will send out workers into his harvest. This section paves the way for Jesus' teaching on discipleship and mission in chapter 10.

Jesus of Nazareth lived with a heart of visceral and profound compassion. A stark contrast to the compassionate heart is poignantly captured in Jesus' parable of the rich man living with a heart of stone. This rich man, "who was dressed in purple and fine linen and who feasted sumptuously every day," was apathetic and blind to the needs of Lazarus, a poor man who lay at his gate, "covered with sores, who longed to satisfy his hunger with what fell from the rich man's table; even the dogs would come and lick his sores" (Luke 16:19–21). The rich man couldn't see Lazarus, his close neighbour living in dehumanizing misery because his heart was rigid, hard, and egocentric. Monopolizing the abundance of possessions, he does not advance life in others. Enslaved by greed, he doesn't comprehend Jesus' wisdom: "Be on your guard against all kinds of greed; for one's life does not consist in the abundance of possessions" (Luke 12:15). While Lazarus was seen as less than human because of his physical condition, the rich man was dehumanized to a much greater extent by his lack of conscience and his insensitivity to his neighbours. The heart of compassion safeguards us from falling into the trap of greed or hiding behind the world of dualism, abstraction, and calculation. Compassion is the core of Christ's love and the guiding light in our becoming the "imitators of God" (Eph. 5:1). "Be merciful, just as your Father is merciful" (Luke 6:36).

The signs of the Anthropocene tell us that humanity does not have a future if we don't make a concerted effort to build a compassionate civilization. Our compassion needs to be directed to both people and nature. A human heart cruel and insensitive to human neighbours will not turn into an eco-sensitive heart overnight. As Archbishop Desmond Tutu said, "Once we start living in a way that is people-friendly to all of God's family, we will also be environment-friendly."[2] Authentic Christian faith can facilitate this process, as it centres on Jesus, who has brought peace on earth that reconciles us to God, to one another, and to all of God's creation (Eph. 1:10; Col 1:15–20). Jesus said, "I came to bring fire to the earth, and how I wish it were already kindled!" (Luke 12:49). The fire of compassion, fostering people's relational power, is the basis of a new civilization celebrating the web of life and conviviality because it can shape a human-friendly and nature-friendly counterculture.

Compassion is the quality of leadership. The reference to "sheep without a shepherd" (Matt. 9:36) evokes the misrule of false shepherds who are unfaithful leaders. It echoes Ezekiel 34, which condemns Israel's false shepherds. They damage the sheep by not strengthening the weak, not healing the sick, not binding up the injured, not bringing back the strayed, and not seeking the lost. They rule people with force and harshness (Ezek. 34:4). False shepherds never search or seek for the scattered sheep to prevent them from becoming food for all the wild animals (Ezek. 34:5–8). Jesus, the true shepherd of his people (Matt. 2:6), is different. The first verb in Matthew 9:35 indicates that Jesus "went about" all the cities and villages (as stated earlier, in 4:23). This verb, the imperfect of the Greek *periagō*, refers to Jesus' repeated or durative action. Jesus did not lead an indifferent and self-absorbed life. He reached out to people on the ground to see their situation with his own eyes. "I myself will search for my sheep and will seek them out" (Ezek. 34:11). Jesus, who is a Davidic shepherd (Ezek. 34:23), is the true God-sent leader.

The November 2021 WCC executive committee statement on the outcome of COP26 urged "all member churches, ecumenical partners and Christian communities to be leaders—not only followers—in making the changes for which we advocate."[3] When the exercise of leadership is urgently required at all

2 Archbishop Desmond Tutu, "Foreword" in *The Green Bible*, (San Francisco: Harper Bibles, 2010), I-13.

3 WCC Executive Committee, "Statement on the Outcome of COP26," 16 November 2021, https://www.oikoumene.org/resources/documents/statement-on-the-outcome-of-cop26.

levels of our communities in the family, church, and society, the quality of leadership matters. It should facilitate the speed of *metanoia* on a civilizational scale and call forth the participation of all. "The creation waits with eager longing for the revealing of the children of God" (Rom. 8:19). The world now waits for the active and diverse contributions of awakened persons from all walks of life who are motivated by conscience and have the courage to change. In line with Jesus' exhortation, we pray to God to send out more workers to expand the urgent ministry of healing, restoration, reconciliation, and unity to transform our wounded world. As the disciples of Jesus, we find ourselves to be summoned to respond to an urgent call to revitalize ministry and mission, filled with the fire of compassion that is ignited by the Jesus movement. To respond to the call, "we intend to stay together."[4] We will continue to pray, work, and move together as we desire to let the world know the presence of God the Immanuel in our midst (Matt. 1:23).

---

4 Message of the 1st Assembly of the World Council of Churches, Amsterdam, the Netherlands, 1948. At the 10th assembly, an invitation to a pilgrimage of justice and peace, was couched as "We intend to move together" ("Message of the 10th Assembly of the WCC," Busan, Republic of Korea, 30 October to 8 November 2013, https://www.oikoumene.org/resources/documents/message-of-the-wcc-10th-assembly.

CHRIST'S LOVE MOVES THE WORLD TO RECONCILIATION AND UNITY

Krzysztof Mielcarek

[25]Just then a lawyer stood up to test Jesus. "Teacher," he said, "what must I do to inherit eternal life?" [26]He said to him, "What is written in the law? What do you read there?" [27]He answered, "You shall love the Lord your God with all your heart, and with all your soul, and with all your strength, and with all your mind; and your neighbour as yourself." [28]And he said to him, "You have given the right answer; do this, and you will live." [29]But wanting to justify himself, he asked Jesus, "And who is my neighbour?" [30]Jesus replied, "A man was going down from Jerusalem to Jericho, and fell into the hands of robbers, who stripped him, beat him, and went away, leaving him half dead. [31]Now, by chance a priest, was going down that road; and when he saw him, he passed by on the other side. [32]So likewise a Levite, when he came to the place and saw him, passed by on the other side. [33]But a Samaritan while travelling came near him; and when he saw him, he was moved with pity. [34]He went to him and bandaged his wounds, having poured oil and wine on them. Then he put him on his own animal, brought him to an inn, and took care of him. [35]The next day he took out two denarii, gave them to the innkeeper, and said, 'Take care of him; and when I come back, I will repay you whatever more you spend.' [36]Which of these three, do you think, was a neighbour to the man who fell into the hands of the robbers?" [37]He said, "The one who showed him mercy." Jesus said to him, "Go and do likewise."

—Luke 10:25–37

"What must I do to inherit eternal life?" "What is written in the law? What do you read there?" Jesus' preliminary dialogue with the scribe brings us to the heart of the pericope we have just read. Since eternal life depends on our love of God and neighbours, for a Christian, there is no more important matter than this commitment. Every devout Israelite recalled this fundamental truth by reciting Shema Israel every day. The scribe, however, takes the dialogue to a new level because he asks Jesus to identify the objects of his love. There is no difficulty with the first because it is God. But who is a neighbour? This question is the core of the parable quoted by Jesus and is intertwined with its central protagonist.

Although biblical tradition has called this story "the parable of the good Samaritan," the figure that unites all its heroes is not a Samaritan, but a poor man who, descending from Jerusalem to Jericho, is attacked by robbers. The parable begins with him, and he is present until the very end. Although the narrator does not tell us this story from his perspective, he is nevertheless at the heart of the parable. It is he who can be identified with the neighbour about whom the scribe asks. To paraphrase other parables of the teacher from Nazareth, one could say that every neighbour in need is like a man attacked by robbers.

By giving this interpretation of a neighbour, Jesus consciously expands the biblical concept of the Hebrew term *rēʼa* or Greek *plesíon*, which usually meant a friend or a neighbour. The story does not, however, mention that the priest, the Levite, or the Samaritan knew the victim in advance. Thus, the main character of the parable meets all the criteria of a stranger.[5] In fact, the construction of the parable gradually strengthens the distance between the attacked one and three passers-by, as verse 30 suggests that he was a Jewish pilgrim returning home after visiting the Sanctuary in Jerusalem. This suggests at least some kind of formal bond between him and the temple staff. Instead, both see him on the road, and they not only pass by but even change to the other side of the road (*antiparerchomai*) so as not to come any closer to the victim of the assault. Thus, they increase their distance from the needy.[6]

On the other hand, the Samaritan is the embodiment of strangeness for the attacked man.[7] The latter, probably a devout Jew, would have treated all Samaritans as renegades.[8] The contempt was mutual; thus, we can point to an extreme distance between the characters. The Samaritan, however, crosses the barrier of hostility and resentment.

Jesus' parable focuses the listener on the Samaritan's actions: he sees a man in need and is moved by his situation. The Samaritan's compassion, however, is not just empty emotion because he takes further concrete actions. He approaches the victim, dresses his wounds, drives him to an inn, nurses him, and pays money toward the further costs of his recovery. Note that Jesus does not share with his listeners the possible happy ending of the story, leaving them in some doubt. Thus, their attention is focused entirely on the attitude of the Samaritan towards the victim—namely, that he did everything he could to take care of this man.

The phrase "everything he could" demands a brief remark. The juxtaposition of the Samaritan with Jesus leads many preachers to exaggerate his merciful attitude as total devotion. However, it is worth noting that the epilogue of the parable brings a different picture. The Samaritan finally resumes his daily activities, leaving the attacked in the care of the inn's owner (10:35). He does not subordinate his whole life to the victim of the robbery but supports the man according to his needs.

What are the consequences of Jesus' message for Christians today? They can be expressed in several points:

1. You may be confronted with a situation in which your neighbour has a sudden need.
2. Belonging to religious institutions does not guarantee a proper attitude towards the needy.
3. Regardless of negative judgments from others, act according to what is good and right.

5 Hebrew: *ben-nēḵar/'iš-noḵri/gēr/zār*; Greek: *allótrios/allogenēs/pároikos*. See Genesis 17:12–27; 42:7; Esther 8:12; 1 Micah 12:10; Job 28:4; Psalm 35:15; 105:12; 109:11; Proverbs 5:10; 8:8; 14:10; 27:2; Ecclesiastes. 6:2; Sirach 32:18; Isaiah 61:5; Jeremiah 14:8; 51:51; Hosea 7:9; 8:7; Joel 4:17; Obadiah 1:11; Ephesians 2:12; 4:18.

6 In the attitude of the priest and the Levite, some see the desire to avoid ritual contamination, while others see it in it disgust for a battered man.

7 Commentators point out that the content of the parable here must have been shocking to Jesus' hearers. There are more such examples in the Gospel of Luke: see, for example, Jesus' cleansing of the lepers (Luke 17:11–19).

8 The origins of the Samaritan people are associated with the conquest of Israel by Assyria (722 BCE). Part of the population of the kingdom was then moved to Mesopotamia, and in its place a foreign population with different culture and beliefs was settled (2 Kings 17:24–41). Over time, they were assimilated, and their beliefs merged with those of the Israelites. This gave rise to an eclectic religion with its center on top of Mount Garizem. The differences between Jews and Samaritans caused mutual resentment (see John 4:9; *Talmud Jerušalaim: Shekalim* 1.4.3; *Shevi'it* 6.1.16; 8.8.1).

4. Help anyone in need, even if this temporarily deprives you of some personal comfort, possessions, or time.
5. Act adequately to meet the needs of your neighbour.

The modern world does not allow us to look at this parable only from the perspective of an individual person. Today, entire nations and even continents are suffering, which calls for a systemic and global response. Many religious and international organizations have been established to help contemporary victims. Huge disparities in wealth and standard of living have caused waves of migration of people in search of better living conditions. A series of bloody regional conflicts have expelled many refugees from their homes. Prosperous countries and regions must, therefore, take deliberate measures to alleviate the misery of the victims of these disastrous phenomena. Recent decades have shown us examples of both unprecedented heroic generosity and cold indifference. We must, therefore, pray that the international community will learn from its mistakes and take effective action. Individual churches, especially those with a global reach, also have an important role.

Nevertheless, the starting point for everyone should be to ask themselves: To what extent am I the neighbour of another person? To what extent am I behaving like a neighbour? Jesus' parable is a kind of cry, a call to us to be a neighbour, even if it means giving up some part of our own comfort, possessions, and time.

Jesus' answer to the scribe's question is, de facto, "EVERYONE." The disciple of Christ is thus called to break down religious, cultural, and political barriers and to reach out to those in need. The theme of this assembly, "The love of Christ moves the world to reconciliation and unity," can thus be paraphrased: "The mercy of Christ leads us to discover our neighbour in every human being."

CHRIST'S LOVE—COMPASSION FOR LIFE—AFFIRMING THE WHOLENESS OF LIFE

Diana Tsaghikyan

[1]As he walked along, he saw a man blind from birth. 2His disciples asked him, "Rabbi, who sinned, this man or his parents, that he was born blind?" 3Jesus answered, "Neither this man nor his parents sinned; he was born blind so that God's works might be revealed in him. 4We must work the works of him who sent me while it is day; night is coming when no one can work. 5As long as I am in the world, I am the light of the world. 6When he had said this, he spat on the ground and made mud with the saliva and spread the mud on the man's eyes, 7saying to him, "Go, wash in the pool of Siloam" (which means Sent). Then he went and washed and came back able to see. 8The neighbours and those who had seen him before as a beggar began to ask, "Is this not the man who used to sit and beg?" 9Some were saying, "It is he." Others were saying, "No, but it is someone like him." He kept saying, "I am the man." 10But they kept asking him, "Then how were your eyes opened?" 11He answered, "The man called Jesus made mud, spread it on my eyes, and said to me, 'Go to Siloam and wash.' Then I went and washed and received my sight." 12They said to him, "Where is he?" He said, "I do not know."

—John 9:1–12

People usually see the healing of the blind man as a miracle. Jesus saw a blind man and, amazingly, enabled that man to see. Indeed, the healing of the blind man was a miracle. Miracles happened then, and miracles happen in various ways today as well. However, this story is not just about a miracle; it is also about Christ's love and the power of compassion.

What do we know about the beggar? This man had parents but was alone; he lived in society but was excluded from it. Blind since birth, he never saw the light until Christ saw him and changed his reality. First, we read that Jesus sees a blind man, and we immediately witness how Jesus rejects the dictum, "The blind and the lame shall not come into the house" (2 Sam. 5:8). Jesus corrects his disciples' misconceptions about sin and suffering, educates them about the work of God, and enlightens them by declaring, "As long as I am in the world, I am the light of the world." Then Jesus makes mud with his saliva, spreads it across the man's eyes, and says, "Go to Siloam and wash." After following those instructions, the beggar returns, able to see.

An incredible miracle has just occurred, but no one seems happy for or interested in the formerly blind man. We witness, perhaps, indifference instead of the needed care and compassion. Interestingly enough, in the questions asked by the others, we do not see a single one that tries to discover his emotions and newly developed feelings. He meets with indifference rather than care and compassion. In contrast, with pure love and grace, Jesus heals a blind man who was excluded and marginalized. Jesus challenges society and acts. He gifts the beggar with a profound feeling of hope and a deeper awareness of God's saving power. He restores the wholeness of the man's life with a new purpose and direction. Jesus gives that man the vision of light.

Disappointment, frustration, and lack of a

vision for life may cloud our present life and future hopes with the darkness of uncertainty, but in a time of darkness, it is imperative to hold a vision of light. We cannot remain in the cave of death, where intelligence is silenced, and no piety or compassion can be found. Today more than ever—after 2022 years—Christian churches still face many challenges. There is a need for precious medication to heal the wounds of Christ's body. Compassion should be the answer.

Genuine compassion has a beautiful significance in the way we treat others. It has the power to move humanity toward a righteous path where Christ's love is elucidated, and the light is seen. Genuine compassion changes the way we live. When we embrace compassion in our lives, we try to be merciful, hopeful, faithful, and patient. In times of impatience, we must remember that God works in mysterious ways. We must value how compassion reminds us of what it means to be human.

Every aspect of this story has spiritual implications; it provides a powerful parallel to the role of God in bringing us to faith and salvation through grace and the power of compassion. Compassion is a fundamental quality of the biblical concept of God. Jesus Christ, in whom God was "revealed in flesh" (1 Tim. 3:16), is an outstanding example of compassion. Jesus taught that compassion should be extended not only to friends and neighbours but to everyone without exception, to the entire human race. The evangelist John wants us to restore and keep our vision of light.

All epochs have their imperatives. In our materialistic and secular age, in the context of a global health pandemic, when we face the horrific reality of racism, discrimination, poverty, violence, political instability, wars, and climate change, it is imperative not to give up. We must value the spiritual aspects of our lives more than ever. Each of us is unique—we have different views, cultures, experiences, and backgrounds—but our mutual faith in Christ, and our love for the Lord, unite us. Above all, there is the unity of service and witness throughout the world in the name of Jesus Christ, who is "the light of the world." Life feels hopeless without a living relationship with our Creator and with each other. Jesus Christ opened the loving path of the blessed life, and this bright, life-giving path will make us strong, confident that each of us has a purpose to live and create. Our Lord Jesus Christ gave humanity the hope and grace to face suffering and inherit eternal life.

I believe that with mutual respect and the firm belief that Christ is risen, we will spread God's word. We will humbly continue to seek the light of God and work toward reconciliation and unity. We will cherish our individual purpose; with this found purpose, we will extend immense respect toward our diverse humanity. Along with this purpose comes the responsibility to act with compassion, with Christ's love in our minds and souls, and with his unwavering light as our guide. However, we cannot accomplish any of these acts on our own: we need each other. Together we may remember our past, live our present, and create our future. We intend to be together—is that not a miracle?

> "Light, and source of illumination,
> housed in unapproachable light. . ..
> In the dawning of morning light,
> bring also the light of understand-
> ing into our souls."[9]

9 Nerses Shnorhali (St Nerses the Graceful) was one of the most remarkable medieval theologians and the ecumenical figure *par excellence* in the history of the Armenian Church. The quotation above is from his "Hymn to the Light" (*Luys ararich Luso*).

CHRIST'S LOVE—TRANSFORMING DISCIPLESHIP—AFFIRMING JUSTICE AND HUMAN DIGNITY

Paulo Ueti

[21] Jesus left that place and went away to the district of Tyre and Sidon. [22]Just then a Canaanite woman from that region came out and started shouting, 'Have mercy on me, Lord, Son of David; my daughter is tormented by a demon.' [23]But he did not answer her at all. And his disciples came and urged him, saying, 'Send her away, for she keeps shouting after us.' [24]He answered, 'I was sent only to the lost sheep of the house of Israel.' [25]But she came and knelt before him, saying, 'Lord, help me.' [26]He answered, 'It is not fair to take the children's food and throw it to the dogs.' [27]She said, 'Yes, Lord, yet even the dogs eat the crumbs that fall from their masters' table.' [28]Then Jesus answered her, 'Woman, great is your faith! Let it be done for you as you wish.' And her daughter was healed instantly.

—Matthew 15:21–28

Matthew's version of this story, with more elements than the version in Mark 7:24–30, is even more provocative because it places Jesus' disciples in the narrative. We know Matthew's Gospel was written around 80–90 CE, reflecting not only the events of Jesus' time in Palestine but what was happening in the church of Syria, the probable origin of most of the writings of this community.

This text is about community. It is about who we welcome and how we welcome them. And being a text about community, it is a provocation about habits of welcoming, reconciliation, and living out unity in Christ Jesus. Different people from different cultures, languages, backgrounds, habits, genders, ages, and positions of power find themselves in a context of gender-based violence, racism, need, pain, illness, exclusion, xenophobia, and established prejudices.

It is always imperative, however, to remind ourselves that God "loves the strangers" (Deut. 10:18). When we read the body of texts in the biblical canon, we notice that the spirit of the Torah and the prophets is very present also in the New Testament, advocating for the protection of people who are facing oppression, illness, exclusion, and violence, who are disadvantaged in the system and experience some kind of need that causes them to be perceived as less human. The poor, strangers, orphans, widows, children, and women are among those who are most to be protected.

The text unfolds the dialogical methodology of a foreign woman in her encounter with Jesus, the Jew. She is Canaanite, a Hellenist by culture. It seems that her being a "foreigner" is relevant to the author of this story. There seems to be a problem in the community regarding dialogue, relationships, and welcoming strangers, foreigners, and women to the communion table. We know that a shared table, *koinonia*, is a proxy for worship, for celebrating and recognizing Jesus walking with us. The shared table heals and brings us all together—or should do so.

We notice the authors' interest in giving prominence to the two women—the daughter and the mother—both nameless. The scene is presented as an encounter, not very friendly at first, between two people who would not normally exchange glances, let alone converse. For many people of that time, non-Jews were considered "dogs," in the same way non-Romans were considered barbarians. Nevertheless, the meeting takes place. There is a debate, apparently between unequals, but when we analyze the discourse, we perceive that the two are on the same level in terms of willingness to engage, technique, and content. The woman is not totally submissive. She is participative, smart, resilient, and persistent in getting what she is after.

The conversation unfolds because of the illness of this woman's daughter, her expectations of Jesus, and her audacity in interrupting Jesus' desire to remain secret. The woman confronts this man who does not want to pay attention to her need, and she faces rudeness and a lack of empathy from the disciples. According to Matthew's text, she "started shouting." Imagine the embarrassing scene of a woman shouting at someone who wanted to remain anonymous. When confronted, Jesus expresses his position, coming from his cultural tradition, what he learned as a child and how he grew up. He resists sharing the bread and the table—a metaphor for the community, a support group. It seems the community of Matthew has a problem regarding who has the right to access the table.

Returning to the storyline, it is interesting to note the issues that permeate the dialogue of these two people from different cultures: an encounter between unequal people; unclean spirit/need; bread above/crumbs below; at the table/under the table. They seem to be talking about different, unrelated subjects. The woman, a Greek by education, has her needs (healing her daughter, casting out the demon, getting her daughter back, getting help, inscribing herself in the linguistic universe of Jesus). Jesus is culturally intransigent (he sounds ethnocentric and intolerant), and he attempts to keep the table inaccessible to her. In Matthew's account, we still have the disciples asking Jesus to "send her away"—which can mean "attend" or "send her away without attending"—but either way, we have intermediaries who are bothered by this relationship. In Matthew's community, it seems that the woman should have no right to access the table, that is, Jesus.

The woman's fundamental question, developed with propriety and rhetorical skill, is: Who has access to Jesus? Who can reach the bread? Is it only the children of Israel, those in Jesus' club and the disciples; those who are prepared; those who are free from sin? The two texts indicate that this was Jesus' initial thought and word. The woman did not accept that cultural and social norm. She did not like living in a world where the norm was to exclude people like her and her kind. She transgressed the homogenous and dominating language of that culture, tradition, and religion and made this man change his mind and attitude. She produced knowledge, laying the foundations of a new epistemological possibility: "Out of the mouths of babes and infants, you have founded a bulwark" (Ps. 8:2a).

It is also interesting, in terms of literary context, that this text is found between two others that mention bread:

Matthew 14:13–21. First sharing of loaves to the 5000; 12 baskets left over.
Matthew 15:21–28. Our conflicting story about who can access Jesus/bread/crumbs.
Matthew 15: 15:32–38. Second sharing of loaves to 4000; 7 baskets left over.

We find the correlation in Mark as well as in Matthew. It seems that the story of the Syrophoenician woman, who argued with Jesus about who could access the bread or obtain healing, resulted in the need to retell the first story of the multiplication of the loaves and give it another ending, affirming that all people have access to Jesus. Here it is good to remember that to have access to Jesus is to have access to the community, to a new project, and to the political and ideo-theological space that goes against the grain of what was established then and also today.

All Have Access To Jesus/Table/Communion/ Community/Dialogue

> There is neither Jew nor Greek, slave nor free, male nor female, all are one in Christ Jesus.
>
> **—Galatians 3:28**

Access to Jesus, to the bread or the crumbs that fall from the table, is related to the meetings and mismatches of people from different cultures, who have different lexicons, and varying needs and desires to learn from each other. This is why our episode places so much emphasis on the culture and geography of the two characters and their needs: the woman and the daughter lacking relationships and participation—bread, table, health, communion, support, recognition—and Jesus and his closest disciples (men, we should mention), trapped by cultural ethnocentrism causing xenophobia and violence. Nonetheless, those men were graced by the ability to listen and, even in disagreement, to overcome their supposed superiority and remain in dialogue until the end. It seems that only in a dialogic process can health and life appear. There may be a warning here for the community that openness to new relationships, spiritual and vocational listening, solidarity, a sense of equity, and sharing are needed to transform disagreements into encounters of love and life. Such encounters prevent illness and death and transform us. In 1 Corinthians 11:28–32, Paul condemned the practice of the supper in the Corinthian community, the eating without prior judgment of oneself. There are many today who are sick and weak; some have already died because the community has not been supportive—hence the exhortation to examine oneself so as not to incur self-condemnation.

We need to "unlearn." "God has chosen what in the world is foolish, even the things that are not, to reduce to nothing the things that are" (1 Cor. 1:27–28). Jesus, or the community, unlearned something in order to apprehend much more. Encounters between different cultures provoke this result when we are truly open and willing to move in the direction of detaching ourselves from our truths, traditions, and certainties. In this way, we can pay attention to the fundamental attitude of our spirituality of liberation: to listen and obey the God who gives life and comes to us in a plural and diverse world.

The woman is not discouraged by the problem of not being attended to. She is a victim, but she is not passive. She has rights, and her awareness of this gives her strength (dynamo) to move forward (face). Even from her condition of "dog" (which she, in effect, claims), she affirms that this is not an issue that can prevent her from fully participating in communion.

This narrative joins others stressing the need for our mentality, theologies, practices, and pastoral care to be anti-racist, anti-xenophobic, and against any kind of violence. Likewise, it calls us to attend unconditionally to those who need help and to pay attention to the conflicts that this may cause in the ecclesial community and also in our common home, the *oikoumene* and the planet. Do we seek dialogue and remain in dialogue even when offended, disqualified, and diminished in our humanity? How can we make this a practice that extends to the environments and contexts in which we live?

Going out to meet others is always a challenge. But it is our call. Are we listening, like the sower in the parable,[10] to the call to sow, no matter how difficult the soil?

May the Trinity bless us with the spirit of indignation and resilience characteristic of our spirituality.

10 Matthew 13:3–8; Mark 4:3–8; Luke 8:5–8.

CHRIST'S LOVE—THE BOND OF CHRISTIAN UNITY AND CHURCHES' COMMON WITNESS

Kenneth Mtata

[20] Then the mother of the sons of Zebedee came to him with her sons, and kneeling before him, she asked a favour of him. [21] And he said to her, "What do you want?" She said to him, "Declare that these two sons of mine will sit, one at your right hand and one at your left, in your kingdom." [22] But Jesus answered, "You do not know what you are asking. Are you able to drink the cup that I am about to drink?" They said to him, "We are able." [23] He said to them, "You will indeed drink my cup, but to sit at my right hand and at my left, this is not mine to grant, but it is for those for whom it has been prepared by my Father." [24] When the ten heard it, they were angry with the two brothers. [25] But Jesus called them to him and said, "You know that the rulers of the Gentiles lord it over them, and their great ones are tyrants over them. [26] It will not be so among you; but whoever wishes to be great among you must be your servant, [27] and whoever wishes to be first among you must be your slave; [28] just as the Son of Man came not to be served but to serve, and to give his life a ransom for many."
—Matthew 20:20–28

The mother of the two sons of Zebedee approaches Jesus in the most reverent posture, close to worship (προσκυνοῦσα), to plead for favour for her two sons. Though the sons are known by the name of their father, Zebedee, she uses her matriarchal authority to plead for their exaltation, typical of those traditional cultures where explicit leadership is patriarchal, but real power is matriarchally determined outside the view of the public. In any case, she is pursuing for her sons what the Gospel of Matthew presents as its ultimate agenda: "But strive first for the kingdom of God and his righteousness, and all these things will be given to you as well" (6:36).

What informs her understanding of the "kingdom"? Some scholars have preferred to read Matthew's reference to the kingdom against the backdrop of the "Jewish Christian community in the process of re-defining its own identity over against Jewish opposition, which was consolidating itself under Pharisaic-scribal leadership."[11] Others see the whole Gospel of Matthew in general and the kingdom language in particular from the broader context of Roman imperial power and domination.[12] The two emphases are not necessarily mutually exclusive. It is known that the Romans, with their concentrated presence in Antioch, informed the social context for the communities behind the gospel of Matthew. These Romans were the "Gentiles" who would immediately come to mind. They exercised domineering power over their colonized subjects through

11 A. B. Du Toit, "The Kingdom of God in the Gospel of Matthew," *Skrif en Kerk* 21, no. 3 (2000), 545.

12 Boris Repschinsk, "Kingdoms of the Earth and the Kingdom of the Heavens: Matthew's Perspective on Political Power," in *The Composition, Theology, and Early Reception of Matthew's Gospel*, ed. Joseph Verheyden, Jens Schröter, and David C. Sim (Tübingen: Mohr Siebeck, 2022), 149.

pliant and surrogate political administration but also through their military presence and religious domination. In this regard, the Romans were indeed exercising "power over" (κατακυριεύουσιν) their subjects. And like all colonized persons, the disciples and their communities were attracted to and mimicked power excesses as demonstrated by the oppressive Romans. It is, therefore, no surprise that they seek to create their own small empires, characterized by domineering "power over" and tyrannical relationships. In this light, the mother of the sons of Zebedee seeks prime positions for her sons. In doing so, she also hopes to guarantee a special place for herself in the kingdom.

In Matthew 20, however, Jesus is offering a reimagination of power as power in sacrificial and humble service (vv. 26–27). It is in such a conception that the kingdom of God is best understood—where greatness is demonstrated by being a servant (διάκονος) and even a slave (δοῦλος), where such service could be unto death. In the immediate literary context of today's passage, Jesus predicts his death (vv. 17–19) and heals the two blind men (contrasted to the two sons of Zebedee?) as he passes through Jericho (vv. 29–34). The death of Jesus is what opens eyes to true greatness. Jesus is not only the teacher but also the ultimate example of *diakonia*, or humble service.

What Does This Mean for Us?

"When the ten heard it, they were angry with the two brothers" (v. 24). Mary Jane Gorman says, "We can identify with the anger of the other ten disciples: If we virtuously resisted asking to sit next to the guest of honor, we might be resentful of someone else who did ask."[13] Just as the unity of disciples was threatened by this act of self-seeking power, so too the unity of the church suffers under the weight of domineering, controlling, and privileged power because, in turn, it generates reactions of anger, jealousy, and mistrust.

Just as in the context of the Roman empire, the world today seems to be burdened by militaristic, exclusivist, idolatrous forms of power. This expression of oppressive power may be perpetuated through deceptive patriarchy and matriarchal alliances (a mother preparing a special place for her sons), absolutist left-wing and right-wing ideologies (one on the right and the other on the left), or race or ethnic nepotistic identities (sons of Zebedee), all in the guise of religiosity and piety (seeking the kingdom of God).

The unity of the church, says Jesus, can be upheld and revitalized through the reversal of such conceptions of power, replacing them with the power of service (*diakonia*). This service is truly unifying if it does not disempower or replace the agency of those on the receiving end. *Diakonia* that serves the unity of the church is carried out in love, sacrificial love. This love must surpass the maternal love for two sons. It is that love with which God loved all humanity. This is love that transcends patriarchal and matriarchal alliances but builds new affiliations of love of brothers and sisters in God's family. It is love that surpasses ideological alliances designed to protect the exclusive privileges of a few. This true love widens the circle to include those who would normally be disqualified. Such love breaks the walls of race and ethnic

13 Mary Jane Gorman, *Watching the Disciples: Learning from Their Mistakes*, (Nashville, TN: Abingdon Press, 2008), https://books.google.co.za/books?id=-ax0qIW55nkC&pg.

bigotry and pride. It is love that humbles without humiliating.

In humility, this love is expressed in the self-sacrificial service of a slave, the *doulos*. The love that adopts this kind of service does not have its base in erotic and passionate feelings. It is not merely filial or based on friendship. It is not necessarily based on parents' love for children or the love of kith and kin. Its fountain must be agape love, the love of all those created in the image of God. This is the love of God shared with us in Christ Jesus. It is this love that can remove the poison of oppressive forms of power in the church and in the world.

The church driven by this love is a powerful witness in the world because it offers an alternative way of exercising power. The church's exercise of power cannot mirror that of the world. It must be salt and light to the world. The church contributes to the transformation of skewed power arrangements in the world through the witness of its members, who live in society as representatives of the coming kingdom of God. Through their exemplary lives and their words, in their families, in their communities, in the church, and in the public sphere, they prevail against the doors of Hades.

The church also witnesses to the world when it unequivocally takes positions that are sometimes unpopular and unsafe. Jesus says, "Let your word be 'Yes, Yes' or 'No, No'; anything more than this comes from the evil one" (Matthew 5:37). The courageous and sacrificial witness of the church aims at resisting, undermining, and ultimately uprooting all systems that generate unjust and unequal power relationships in the world and in the church. Faithful churches should be able to say: "It shall not be so among us!" Churches shall say so at local, regional, national, and global levels. The church shall say "No" to growing militarism, non-productive markets, materialism, monoculturalism, manipulation, misinformation, malice, mob justice, and the growing monopoly over the public and the commons. In the same vein, the church shall shout an emphatic "YES!" It says yes to mercy and compassion, to meaningful relationships, to multilateral cooperation of nations, to mediated solutions to conflict, to moderation of positions, and to mutuality. This is the rearrangement of power to which Jesus is calling us!

CONTRIBUTORS

The Rev. Dr **Hyunju Bae** is a former professor at Busan Presbyterian University in the Republic of Korea and an ordained minister in the Presbyterian Church of Korea. She has served on the executive and central committees of the World Council of Churches in the period from Busan to Karlsruhe. She is Co-President of Korea Christian Environmental Movement Solidarity for Integrity of Creation.

Archimandrite Prof. Dr **Jack Khalil** from the Greek Orthodox Patriarchate of Antioch and All the East, is dean of the St. John of Damascus Institute of Theology, University of Balamand, and Professor of New Testament Studies. He holds a PhD from the Aristotle University of Thessaloniki and studied for three years as a visiting fellow at the Eberhard-Karls-Universität in Tübingen, Germany. He is a member of the WCC Central Committee and the Commission on Faith and Order.

Dr **Krzysztof Mielcarek** is a theologian, biblical scholar, and associate professor of the Faculty of Theology in the John Paul II Catholic Theology of Lublin (Poland). He is one of the editors and translators of the Polish Ecumenical Bible (2017). He has been a Roman Catholic commissioner in the Faith and Order Commission of the World Council of Churches since 2014.

Rev. Dr **Kenneth Mtata** is a Zimbabwean theologian and the general secretary of the Zimbabwe Council of Churches. He has worked on hermeneutics, the church in public engagement, and the interface of religion and social transformation. His PhD at the University of KwaZulu-Natal was on Space and Place in the Gospel of John.

Dr **Diana Tsaghikyan** is an assistant professor at the Faculty of Theology, Yerevan State University, and the head of the undergraduate program. She also serves as a member of the PhD thesis committee at the Gevorkian Theological Seminary (University), Mother See of Holy Etchmiadzin. Dr Tsaghikyan joined the WWC in 2019 as a representative of the Armenian Apostolic Church (Mother See of Holy Etchmiadzin) and a member of the central committee. She received her PhD and MTh from the University of Edinburgh, MA in Religious Studies from the Central Baptist Theological Seminary in KS, USA, and BA from the Yerevan State University of Languages and Social Sciences. Dr Tsaghikyan's central research focuses on patristic studies and the Christian doctrine. She is particularly interested in the theological literature of Armenian church fathers. Further research interests include ecumenical studies and contemporary issues in theology

Dr **Paulo Ueti** is a Brazilian with a Japanese mother and an Italian father. He is a student of Latin American theologies, Contextual Bible Studies, the New Testament canon and its relation to church history and empire theologies, spirituality, gender, environmental justice, and ecclesiology. He is a member of the Ecumenical Centre for Biblical Studies (CEBI) from the Episcopal Anglican Church of Brazil, working in London at the Anglican Communion Office with Anglican Alliance (Development, Relief and Advocacy) and the Department of Theological Education.

INHALT

EINLEITUNG

Die Bibelarbeit für thematische Plenarsitzungen stellen einen wichtigen Aspekt der Arbeit der Vollversammlung dar. Sie geben den Teilnehmenden Gelegenheit, sich täglich zum Studium einer Bibelstelle zu treffen, um über das Thema und das Erlebnis der Vollversammlung zu reflektieren. Gemeinsam können sich die Teilnehmenden ein Urteil darüber bilden, welche Aufgabe Gott ihnen und der ökumenischen Bewegung zugedacht hat. Sie treffen sich dazu in Gruppen, die klein genug sind, dass alle etwas dazu beisteuern können, und groß genug, um eine Reihe von Blickwinkeln abzubilden.

Die Gespräche zur Bibelarbeit geben den Teilnehmenden Gelegenheit, gemeinsam dem Thema der Vollversammlung anhand von biblischen Texten, Kenntnissen und Erfahrungen nachzugehen. Die Beteiligung an der Bibelarbeit in der Gruppe bedeutet, offen zu sein füreinander sowie für die Bibelstelle und den Heiligen Geist. Es geht nicht darum, eine Debatte zu gewinnen oder die anderen von einer bestimmten Ansicht zu überzeugen. Diese Sitzungen sollen ein Ort sein, an dem die Teilnehmenden all das, was sie in der Vollversammlung gehört und getan haben, einordnen und gemeinsam die Möglichkeiten zur Verwandlung entdecken können, die Gott uns bietet.

ÜBERSICHT

Tag 2, Donnerstag, 1. September 2022

Tagesthema: *Der Zweck von Gottes Liebe in Christus für die ganze Schöpfung – Versöhnung und Einheit*
Bibelstellen: Kol 1;19 f. (Eph 1;10) und Mt 9;35 f. (Die Barmherzigkeit Christi)
Thema im Plenum: *Der Zweck von Gottes Liebe wiedergeboren in Jesus Christus – Versöhnung und Einheit*
Betrachtungen von: Pater Jack Khalil und Pfarrerin Dr. Hyunju Bae

Tag 3, Freitag, 2. September 2022

Tagesthema: *Europa*
Bibelstellen: Lukas 10;25-37 (Der barmherzige Samariter)
Thema im Plenum: *Europa*
Betrachtungen von: Prof. Dr. Krzysztof Mielcarek (Polen/Europa)

Tag 6, Montag, 5. September 2022

Tagesthema: *Die Liebe Christi – Barmherzigkeit für das Leben*
Bibelstellen: Johannes 9;1-12
Thema im Plenum: *Bejahung der Ganzheit des Lebens*
Betrachtungen von: Prof. Dr. Diana Tsaghikyan (Europa)

Tag 7, Dienstag, 6. September 2022

Tagesthema: *Die Liebe Christi – Verwandelnde Nachfolge*
Bibelstellen: Matthäus 15;21-28 (Die kanaanäische Frau)
Thema im Plenum: *Bejahung von Gerechtigkeit und Menschenwürde*

Betrachtungen von: Dr. Paulo Ueti (Brasilien/Südamerika)

Tag 8, Mittwoch, 7. September 2022
Tagesthema: *Die Liebe Christi – Das Band der christlichen Einheit und das gemeinsame Zeugnis der Kirchen*
Bibelstellen: Matthäus 20;20-28
Thema im Plenum: *Christliche Einheit und das gemeinsame Zeugnis der Kirchen*
Betrachtungen von: Pfarrer Dr. Kenneth Mtata (Simbabwe/Afrika)

Lasset uns füreinander beten, während wir uns auf diese Aufgabe vorbereiten und an der Vollversammlung teilnehmen. Lasst *die Liebe Christi die Welt bewegen, versöhnen und einen.*

DER ZWECK VON GOTTES LIEBE IN CHRISTUS FÜR DIE GANZE SCHÖPFUNG—VERSÖHNUNG UND EINHEIT

Jack Khalil

[19] Denn es hat Gott gefallen, alle Fülle in ihm wohnen zu lassen [20] und durch ihn alles zu versöhnen zu ihm hin, es sei auf Erden oder im Himmel, indem er Frieden machte durch sein Blut am Kreuz.
—Kolosser 1;19–20

Diese Verse sind Teil des Christushymnus in Kolosser 1;15–20. Unabhängig davon, ob diese Textstelle aus einem überlieferten älteren Hymnus stammt oder von Paulus selbst im Stile einer Hymne geschrieben wurde, klingt sie wie Musik in den Ohren all jener, die Gott lieben. Indem sie den Erlöser der Welt als den Schöpfer erkennt, der alles ins Leben gerufen hat, stellt sie eine Verbindung her zwischen der göttlichen Heilsökonomie und der Schöpfungslehre. Die erste Strophe (Verse 15-18a) offenbart, dass Christus mit dem Schöpfer aller Dinge „im Himmel und auf Erden" (V. 16) identisch ist und wechselt am Schluss zu Ihm, der das Haupt der Kirche ist (V. 18a). Die zweite Strophe (Verse 18b-20) enthüllt die Wohltätigkeit Christi gegenüber der gesamten Schöpfung „es sei auf Erden oder im Himmel" (V. 20), wie sie durch seine Menschwerdung (V. 19), seine Leidensgeschichte, seinen Tod und seine Auferstehung allen Menschen bewiesen wurde. Hieran wird deutlich, dass die in der zweiten Strophe angesprochenen vergangenen Ereignisse in engem Zusammenhang mit den Zusicherungen aus der ersten Strophe stehen: nämlich, dass Christus der Schöpfer von allem ist. Die Liebe Christi, die sich darin offenbart, dass durch sein Blut alles versöhnt wird zu ihm hin, wurzelt in Seiner Liebe, die er bei der Schöpfung aller Dinge zeigte. Die Wiederholung des Ausdrucks „alles … im Himmel und auf Erden"—sowohl in der ersten Strophe, in der es um die Schöpfung aller Dinge geht, als auch in der zweiten Strophe, in der es um aller Versöhnung geht—bestätigt die vorherige Anmerkung, dass die Versöhnung von allem aus der Liebe Christi zu allem, was er erschaffen hat, herrührt. Die Liebe Christi dauert von Ewigkeit zu Ewigkeit. Er umsorgt und behütet alles auf Erden wie im Himmel, denn alles ist Seins.

Die Liebe Christi ruft uns und bewegt uns zur Versöhnung. Sie ruft uns dazu auf, unsere Feindschaft gegen Ihn (V. 21) zu bereuen, die sich in bösen Taten gegen unsere Nächsten und gegen sein Universum zeigt. Es hilft, wenn wir uns bewusst machen, dass unsere Sünde gegen Gott nicht auf Blasphemie und Undankbarkeit beschränkt ist, sondern hauptsächlich durch Versündigung in zwischenmenschlichen Beziehungen und gegen die Umwelt erfolgt.

Laut Römer 8;7 ist Feindschaft eine Folge davon, dass „das Fleisch sich dem Gesetz Gottes nicht unterwirft", das heißt, wenn man danach strebt, sich selbst und das eigene selbstsüchtige Begehren zum Nachteil unserer Mitmenschen zufriedenzustellen (Gal. 5;16). „Götzendienst, Zauberei, Feindschaft, Hader, Eifersucht, Zorn, Zank, Zwietracht, Spaltungen" (Gal. 5;20) als Werke des Fleisches sind nur einige ausgewählte Beispiele für Sünden in Beziehungen. In diesem Sinne heißt es in Kolosser 1;21, dass die Menschen in bösen Werken Gott feindlich gesinnt seien.

Die Tatsache, dass Sünde und böse Werke Menschen zu Feinden Gottes machen, heißt weder, dass Sünde zu einer auf Gegenseitigkeit beruhenden Feindschaft zwischen Gott und der Menschheit führt, noch, dass Gott den Sündigen feindlich gesinnt ist. Eine solche Einstellung ist nirgends in den Episteln von Paulus zu finden. Im Gegenteil, wer wem gegenüber feindlich gesinnt ist, macht Paulus sehr deutlich, wenn er sagt, „Feindschaft gegen Gott, weil das Fleisch sich dem Gesetz Gottes nicht unterwirft" (Röm. 8;7) und man sei feindlich „gesinnt in bösen Werken" (Kol. 1;21).

Der heilige Johannes Chrysostomos drückt das genauer aus: „Und was ermahnt er? ‚Versöhnt euch mit Gott!' Es heißt nicht: Versöhnet Gott mit euch, denn nicht Gott hält Feindschaft, sondern ihr; denn Gott hält niemals Feindschaft."[1] Tatsächlich zeigen sowohl die aktive Form „versöhnen" (καταλλάξαι oder ἀποκαταλλάξαι), die im Brief an die Kolosser 1;20 und an anderen Stellen verwendet wird, wenn Paulus über die Werke Gottes schreibt, als auch die passive Form „versöhnt werden" (καταλλάττεσθαι), die verwendet wird, wenn Paulus die Christinnen und Christen ermahnt, mit Gott versöhnt zu werden, ohne jeglichen Zweifel, dass Gott sich mit uns versöhnt hat.

Gott versöhnt jene, die zu Feinden Gottes wurden, die Gott gegenüber Undankbarkeit zeigten. Und das taten sie immer dann, wenn sie zu Konflikten und Kriegen, zu wachsenden sozialen und wirtschaftlichen Ungleichheiten, zur Klimakrise und zur COVID-19-Pandemie beitrugen. Die Vergebung der Feindschaft durch den Tod und die Auferstehung Christi schuf Frieden mit allen Menschen, die durch solche sündigen Werke zu Feinden wurden.

Nur der menschgewordene Sohn, von dem es heißt „es hat Gott gefallen, alle Fülle in ihm wohnen zu lassen" (Kol. 1;19), kann den Frieden wiederherstellen, wo Feindschaft herrscht, kann wieder Gerechtigkeit walten lassen, wo noch immer viele unter Ungerechtigkeit leiden, kann wieder für Einheit sorgen zwischen den Menschen, die von „„Götzendienst, Zauberei, Feindschaft, Hader, Eifersucht, Zorn, Zank, Zwietracht, Spaltungen" vernebelt sind.

Die Menschen hätten es nie von sich aus geschafft, die zur Versöhnung mit Gott erforderliche Gerechtigkeit zu erlangen. Unter dieser Voraussetzung verbindet der Apostel Paulus in Vers 20 den Moment der Versöhnung mit dem Tod Christi am Kreuz („durch sein Blut am Kreuz").

Weil das göttliche Blut, das für uns am Kreuz vergossen wurde, die Macht hat, Feindschaft zu vergeben, schuf es Frieden mit allem, das „sei auf Erden oder im Himmel". Auf die gleiche Weise bringen der erlösende Tod und die heilsstiftende Auferstehung Christi allen die Einheit, die von der Liebe Christi bewegt werden. Wer die selbstsüchtige Liebe, die Wurzel aller Sünde, zurückweist und aus der Liebe Christi und Seiner selbstlosen Hingabe lernt, wird durch Christus auch mit allen anderen versöhnt. Die Güte und Barmherzigkeit Christi erwidern sie mit Liebe, Gerechtigkeit und Frieden, die sie als Grundsätze für ihr Verhalten gegenüber „allen Dingen" und allen Menschen annehmen, die Christus liebt und für die er gestorben ist.

Heute sind wir aufgerufen, gemeinsam für die Liebe Christi zu danken, die er unserer Welt und allen Menschen entgegenbringt, und im Gebet

1 St. Johannes Chrysostom, „Homilien über den zweiten Brief an die Korinther", in *New Advent*, https://www.newadvent.org/fathers/2202.htm

reumütig über unsere konkrete Erwiderung auf seine Liebe nachzudenken. Mit ganzem Herzen wollen wir vom Blut am Kreuze lernen, dass wir alle Opfer bringen müssen, und gemeinsam etwas für Gerechtigkeit, Frieden und Versöhnung durch Christus, unseren gesegneten Herrn der Herrlichkeit, tun.

1. Wie bewegt uns die Liebe Christi zu Gerechtigkeit und zur Einheit? Was lernen wir von Seiner Liebe?
2. Wie können wir uns als Antwort auf Gottes Liebe dankbar zeigen? Was sind konkrete Taten der Liebe gegenüber Menschen und der ganzen Schöpfung, zu denen uns Gott bewegt?

DER ZWECK VON GOTTES LIEBE IN CHRISTUS FÜR DIE GANZE SCHÖPFUNG— VERSÖHNUNG UND EINHEIT

Hyunju Bae

[35] Und Jesus zog umher in alle Städte und Dörfer, lehrte in ihren Synagogen und predigte das Evangelium von dem Reich und heilte alle Krankheiten und alle Gebrechen. [36] Und als er das Volk sah, jammerte es ihn; denn sie waren geängstet und zerstreut wie die Schafe, die keinen Hirten haben. [37] Da sprach er zu seinen Jüngern: Die Ernte ist groß, aber wenige sind der Arbeiter. [38] Darum bittet den Herrn der Ernte, dass er Arbeiter in seine Ernte sende.

—Matthäus 9;35–38

Jesus der Barmherzige

Matthäus 9;35–38 ist ein Scheideweg. Der Text blickt zurück auf das geistliche Wirken Jesu und nimmt auch Seine Lehren zur Mission der Jünger vorweg. Vers 35 fasst das Wirken Jesu aus Matthäus 4;23 durch Wiederholung von Worten wie „lehrte", „predigte" und „heilte" zusammen. Diese Tätigkeiten nennt man auch das Dreifache Amt Christi. Jesus erleuchtete den Geist der Menschen, forderte sie auf, ihre Herzen für das Kommen von Gottes Herrschaft zu öffnen, und heilte ihre körperlichen Gebrechen.

Vers 36 offenbart, dass Barmherzigkeit die treibende Kraft hinter dem geistlichen Wirken Jesu ist. Jesus hatte Mitgefühl mit den Menschen, die geängstet und zerstreut waren. „Geängstet" (*eskylmenoi*) bedeutete ursprünglich geschunden oder gehäutet. „Zerstreut" (*errimmenoi*) bedeutet ausgestreckt oder auf dem Boden liegend. Die Menschen wurden ausgebeutet, waren entmutigt, erschöpft, geknechtet, niedergeschmettert. Diesen Menschen, die wie Schafe ohne Hirte waren, begegnete Jesus mit Barmherzigkeit. Das griechisches Verb *splagchnizomai*, mit dem in Matthäus die Barmherzigkeit Jesu beschrieben wird (14;14; 15;32; 18;27; 20;34), stammt vom Substantiv *splagchnon*, das folgende Bedeutungen hat: 1. die inneren Teile eines Körpers bzw. die Eingeweide; 2. das Herz und 3. Liebe oder Zuneigung. Die Barmherzigkeit, die Jesus in seinen Gnadenakten (5;7; 9;13) zeigte, floss spontan aus dem Vermögen der Liebe, aus dem Bauch heraus zu fühlen und Mitleid zu haben, das heißt Herz und Leib gesamtheitlich einzubinden. Im Grund genommen ist die Barmherzigkeit Urheberin des Dreifachen Amtes Christi.

In 9;37 zeigt Jesus seinen Sinn für Realität, als er das unausgewogene Verhältnis zwischen einer großen Ernte und wenigen Arbeitskräften erkennt. Das führt jedoch nicht zu Verzweiflung, sondern dazu, sich der der großartigen Gelegenheit bewusst zu werden und zum Gebet. Im nächsten Vers hält Jesus seine Jünger zum Beten an, damit der Herr der Ernte Arbeiter in seine Ernte sende. Dieser Abschnitt bereitet den Weg für die Lehren Jesu über Nachfolge und Mission in Kapitel 10.

Jesus von Nazareth lebte mit einem Herzen voll tiefgehender und inniger Barmherzigkeit. Einen krassen Gegensatz zum barmherzigen Herzen fängt Jesus eindringlich im Gleichnis vom reichen Mann ein, der mit einem Herzen aus Stein lebt. Der reiche Mann, „der [sich] kleidete in Purpur und kostbares Leinen und lebte alle Tage herrlich und in Freuden", war gleichgültig und blind gegenüber der Not von Lazarus, einem armen Mann, der vor seiner Tür lag, „voll [war] von Geschwüren und begehrte sich zu sättigen von dem, was von des Reichen Tisch fiel, doch kamen die Hunde und leckten an seinen Geschwüren" (Lukas 16;19-21). Der reiche Mann konnte Lazarus nicht sehen, seinen unmittelbaren Nächsten, der in entmenschlichendem Elend lebte, denn sein Herz war unbeugsam, hart und egozentrisch. Er hortet ein Übermaß an Besitztümern, wodurch er das Leben anderer nicht besser macht. Als Sklave der Habgier versteht er die Weisheit Jesu nicht: „Seht zu und hütet euch vor aller Habgier; denn niemand lebt davon, dass er viele Güter hat" (Lukas 12;15). Während man Lazarus wegen seines körperlichen Zustands für weniger menschlich hielt, wurde der Reiche durch seinen Mangel an Gewissen und seine Gefühllosigkeit gegenüber seinem Nächsten in wesentlich höherem Maße entmenschlicht. Ein Herz voll Barmherzigkeit bewahrt uns davor, in die Falle der Habgier zu tappen oder uns hinter einer Welt aus Dualismus, Ablenkung und Berechnung zu verstecken. Barmherzigkeit bildet den Kern der Liebe Christi und das Leitbild auf unserem Weg, „Gott nachzuahmen" (Eph. 5;1). „Seid barmherzig, wie auch euer Vater barmherzig ist" (Lukas 6;36).

Die Anzeichen des Anthropozäns sagen uns, dass die Menschheit keine Zukunft hat, wenn wir uns nicht gemeinsam darum bemühen, eine barmherzige Zivilisation aufzubauen. Unsere Barmherzigkeit muss sowohl für Menschen als auch für die Natur gelten. Ein Menschenherz, das seinen menschlichen Nächsten gegenüber unbarmherzig und gefühllos ist, wird sich nicht über Nacht in ein ökologisch sensibles Herz verwandeln. Dazu sagte Erzbischof Desmond Tutu: „Sobald wir anfangen so zu leben, dass es für alle Menschen aus Gottes Familie verträglich ist, werden wir auch umweltverträglich sein."[2] Diesen Prozess kann ein wahrhaftiger christlicher Glaube begünstigen, da bei diesem Jesus im Mittelpunkt steht, der Frieden auf Erden gebracht hat, der uns zu Gott, zu einander und zur ganzen Schöpfung Gottes hin versöhnt (Eph. 1;10; Kol. 1;15–20). Jesus sprach: „Ich bin gekommen, Feuer auf die Erde zu werfen; was wollte ich lieber, als dass es schon brennte!" (Lukas 12;49). Das Feuer der Barmherzigkeit, das den Menschen die Kraft zur Beziehungsfähigkeit gibt, bildet die Grundlage für eine neue Zivilisation, die das Geflecht des Lebens und die Konvivenz feiert, denn sie kann eine Gegenkultur formen, die für Mensch und Natur verträglich ist.

Barmherzigkeit ist eine Führungsqualität. Der Verweis auf „Schafe, die keinen Hirten haben" (Matt. 9;36) erzeugt die Vorstellung von schlechter Herrschaft durch falsche Hirten, die untreue Anführer sind. Darin klingt Hesekiel 34 nach, wo Israels falsche Hirten verdammt werden. Sie schaden den Schafen, weil sie das Schwache nicht stärken, das Kranke nicht heilen, das Verwundete nicht verbinden, das Verirrte nicht zurückbringen und das Verlorene nicht suchen. Sie herrschen mit Zwang und Härte über die Menschen (Hes. 34;4). Falsche Hirten suchen nicht nach den zerstreuten Schafen, damit diese nicht allen wilden Tieren zum Fraß werden (Hes. 34;5–8). Jesus, der wahre Hirte seiner Leute (Matt. 2;6), ist anders. Das erste Verb in Matthäus 9;35 gibt an, dass Jesus „umherzog" in alle Städte und Dörfer (wie schon zuvor in 4;23 erwähnt). Dieses Verb, das Imperfekt des griechischen *periagō*, weist darauf hin, dass Jesus

2 Erzbischof Desmond Tutu, „Vorwort" in *The Green Bible*, (San Francisco: Harper Bibles, 2010), I-13.

dies immer wieder bzw. ständig tat. Jesus führte kein gleichgültiges und selbstsüchtiges Leben. Er trat mit den Menschen vor Ort in Kontakt, um sich ein eigenes Bild von ihrer Situation zu machen. „Siehe, ich will mich meiner Herde selbst annehmen und sie suchen" (Hes. 34;11). Jesus, der ein Hirte im Sinne Davids ist (Hes. 34;23), ist der wahre von Gott gesandte Fürst.

In der im November 2021 vom ÖRK-Exekutivausschuss veröffentlichen Erklärung zu den Ergebnissen der Weltklimakonferenz COP26 wurden „alle Mitgliedskirchen, ökumenischen Partner und christlichen Gemeinschaften" nachdrücklich aufgefordert, „voranzugehen (und nicht nur zu folgen) und die Veränderungen umzusetzen, für die wir uns stark machen. "[3] Wenn auf allen Ebenen unserer Gemeinden in Familie, Kirche und Gesellschaft dringend Führung übernommen werden muss, dann ist die Führungsqualität von Bedeutung. Diese muss das Tempo der *Metanoia* im zivilisatorischen Rahmen fördern und alle dazu bringen mitzumachen. „Denn das ängstliche Harren der Kreatur wartet darauf, dass die Kinder Gottes offenbar werden" (Röm. 08;19). Die Welt wartet jetzt auf die aktiven und vielfältigen Beiträge erweckter Menschen aus allen Gesellschaftsschichten, deren Gewissen sie dazu treibt und die den Mut haben, etwas zu verändern. Angelehnt an die Ermahnungen Jesu beten wir zu Gott, uns mehr Arbeiter zu senden, die das dringliche Amt von Heilung, Erneuerung, Versöhnung und Einheit auf die Verwandlung unserer verwundeten Welt ausweiten. Als Nachfolgende Jesu sind wir aufgefordert, erfüllt vom Feuer der Barmherzigkeit, das die Jesus-Bewegung. entfacht hat, auf den drängenden Ruf nach Wiederbelebung von Amt und Mission zu antworten. „Wir wollen zusammenbleiben"[4], um dem Ruf zu folgen. Wir werden weiterhin gemeinsam beten, arbeiten und unterwegs sein, da wir der Welt Kenntnis geben wollen von der Gegenwart Gottes, des Immanuel, in unserer Mitte (Matt. 1;23).

---

3 ÖRK-Exekutivausschuss, „Erklärung - Ergebnis von COP26", 16. November 2021, https://www.oikoumene.org/de/resources/documents/statement-on-the-outcome-of-cop26.

4 Botschaft der 1. Vollversammlung des Ökumenischen Rats der Kirchen, Amsterdam, Niederlande, 1948. Auf der 10. Vollversammlung wurde durch die Formulierung „Wir wollen den Weg gemeinsam fortsetzen" eine Einladung zu einem Pilgerweg der Gerechtigkeit und des Friedens ausgedrückt („Botschaft der 10. ÖRK-Vollversammlung", Busan, Republik Korea, 30. Oktober bis 8. November 2013, https://www.oikoumene.org/de/resources/documents/message-of-the-wcc-10th-assembly.)

DIE LIEBE CHRISTI BEWEGT DIE WELT ZUR VERSÖHNUNG UND EINHEIT

Krzysztof Mielcarek

[25]Und siehe, da stand ein Gesetzeslehrer auf, versuchte ihn und sprach: Meister, was muss ich tun, dass ich das ewige Leben ererbe? [26]Er aber sprach zu ihm: Was steht im Gesetz geschrieben? Was liest du? [27]Er antwortete und sprach: »Du sollst den Herrn, deinen Gott, lieben von ganzem Herzen, von ganzer Seele und mit all deiner Kraft und deinem ganzen Gemüt, und deinen Nächsten wie dich selbst« (5. Mose 6,5; 3. Mose 19,18). [28]Er aber sprach zu ihm: Du hast recht geantwortet; tu das, so wirst du leben. [29]Er aber wollte sich selbst rechtfertigen und sprach zu Jesus: Wer ist denn mein Nächster? [30]Da antwortete Jesus und sprach: Es war ein Mensch, der ging von Jerusalem hinab nach Jericho und fiel unter die Räuber; die zogen ihn aus und schlugen ihn und machten sich davon und ließen ihn halb tot liegen. [31]Es traf sich aber, dass ein Priester dieselbe Straße hinabzog; und als er ihn sah, ging er vorüber. [32]Desgleichen auch ein Levit: Als er zu der Stelle kam und ihn sah, ging er vorüber. [33]Ein Samariter aber, der auf der Reise war, kam dahin; und als er ihn sah, jammerte es ihn; [34]und er ging zu ihm, goss Öl und Wein auf seine Wunden und verband sie ihm, hob ihn auf sein Tier und brachte ihn in eine Herberge und pflegte ihn. [35]Am nächsten Tag zog er zwei Silbergroschen heraus, gab sie dem Wirt und sprach: Pflege ihn; und wenn du mehr ausgibst, will ich dir's bezahlen, wenn ich wiederkomme. [36]Wer von diesen dreien, meinst du, ist der Nächste geworden dem, der unter die Räuber gefallen war? [37]Er sprach: Der die Barmherzigkeit an ihm tat. Da sprach Jesus zu ihm: So geh hin und tu desgleichen!

—Lukas 10;25–37—Luke 10:25–37

„Was muss ich tun, dass ich das ewige Leben ererbe?" „Was steht im Gesetz geschrieben? Was liest du?" Der einleitende Dialog zwischen Jesus und dem Schriftgelehrten bringt uns zum Kern der Perikope, die wir gerade gelesen haben. Da das ewige Leben von unserer Liebe zu Gott und unseren Nächsten abhängt, gibt es für einen Mensch christlichen Glaubens nichts Wichtigeres als diese Verpflichtung. Jeder gläubige Israelit gedachte dieser grundlegenden Wahrheit durch das tägliche Rezitieren des Shema Jisrael. Doch der Schriftgelehrte treibt den Dialog noch einen Schritt weiter, denn er bittet Jesus, die Objekte seiner Liebe zu bestimmen. Das erste Objekt stellt keine Schwierigkeit dar, denn das ist Gott. Doch wer ist ein Nächster? Diese Frage bildet den Kernpunkt des von Jesus erzählten Gleichnisses und ist eng mit ihrem Hauptprotagonisten verbunden.

Obwohl diese Geschichte in der biblischen Tradition „Gleichnis vom barmherzigen Samariter" heißt, handelt es sich bei der Person, die alle Hauptfiguren verbindet, nicht um einen Samariter, sondern um einen armen Mann, der von Jerusalem nach Jericho hinabging und unter die Räuber fiel. Das Gleichnis beginnt mit ihm, und er ist bis zum Schluss anwesend. Obwohl uns diese Geschichte nicht aus seiner Perspektive geschildert wird, steht er doch im Mittelpunkt des Gleichnisses. Ihn kann man mit dem Nächsten gleichsetzen, nach dem der

Schriftgelehrte fragt. Anders ausgedrückt könnte man anhand der anderen Gleichnisse des Lehrers aus Nazareth sagen, dass jeder Nächste in Not so ist wie ein Mann, der unter die Räuber fiel.

Durch diese Interpretation eines Nächsten erweitert Jesus bewusst den biblischen Begriff des hebräischen Ausdrucks *rēʻa* oder auf Griechisch *plesíon*, mit dem normalerweise ein Freund oder Nachbar gemeint ist. Doch in der Geschichte wird nicht erwähnt, dass der Priester, der Levit oder der Samariter das Opfer vorher schon kannten. Deshalb treffen auf die Hauptfigur des Gleichnisses alle Kriterien eines Fremden zu.[5] Tatsächlich vergrößert der Aufbau des Gleichnisses nach und nach die Distanz zwischen dem Angegriffenen und den drei Vorübergehenden, denn Vers 30 weist darauf hin, dass es sich bei ihm um einen jüdischen Pilger handelte, der sich nach dem Besuch des Heiligtums in Jerusalem auf dem Heimweg befand. Das deutet zumindest auf eine Art formeller Verbindung zwischen ihm und dem Personal im Tempel hin. Stattdessen sehen ihn beide auf der Straße und sie gehen nicht nur vorüber, sondern wechseln auch noch auf die andere Straßenseite (*antiparerchomai*), damit sie nur ja nicht in die Nähe des angegriffenen Opfers kommen. Dadurch vergrößern sie ihre Distanz zu dem Bedürftigen.[6]

Auf der anderen Seite stellt der Samariter für den angegriffenen Mann die Verkörperung der Fremdartigkeit dar.[7] Letzterer, vermutlich ein frommer Jude, hätte alle Samariter als Abtrünnige.[8] Der Hass beruhte auf Gegenseitigkeit, daher können wir auf eine extreme Distanz zwischen den Personen verweisen. Der Samariter überschreitet jedoch die Barriere aus Feindseligkeit und Groll.

Das Gleichnis Jesu lenkt die Aufmerksamkeit der Zuhörenden auf die Taten des Samariters: er sieht einen Mann in Not und wird von dessen Situation bewegt. Doch bei der Barmherzigkeit des Samariters handelt es sich nicht bloß um ein bedeutungsloses Gefühl, denn er unternimmt weitere konkrete Maßnahmen. Er geht zu dem Opfer hin, verbindet die Wunden des Mannes, bringt ihn in eine Herberge, pflegt ihn und bezahlt die weiteren Kosten für seine Genesung im Voraus. Beachten Sie, dass Jesus seinen Zuhörenden nicht den möglicherweise glücklichen Ausgang der Geschichte erzählt, sondern sie darüber im Unklaren lässt. So konzentriert sich ihre Aufmerksamkeit gänzlich auf die Haltung des Samariters gegenüber dem Opfer—nämlich, dass er alles tat, was er konnte, um für diesen Mann zu sorgen.
Der Satzteil „alles, was er konnte“ verlangt nach einer kurzen Anmerkung. Die

5 Hebräisch: *ben-nēkar/ʼiš-nokri/gēr/zār*; Griechisch: *allótrios/allogenēs/pároikos*. Siehe 1. Mose 17;12–27, 42;7; Ester 8;12; 1 Micha 12:10; Hiob 28;4; Psalm 35;15, 105;12, 109;11; Sprüche 5;10, 8;8, 14;10, 27;2; Prediger 6;2; Sirach 32;18; Jesaja 61;5; Jeremia 14;8, 51;51; Hosea 7;9, 8;7, Joel 4;17; Obadja 1;11; Epheser 2;12, 4;18.

6 In der Haltung des Priesters und des Leviten sehen manche den Wunsch, eine rituelle Verunreinigung zu vermeiden, während andere darin Abscheu für einen geschlagenen Mann sehen.

7 Exegeten weisen darauf hin, dass der Inhalt des vorliegenden Gleichnisses für die Menschen, die Jesus zuhörten, schockierend gewesen sein muss. Im Lukas-Evangelium gibt noch mehr solcher Beispiele: siehe zum Beispiel die Reinigung der Aussätzigen durch Jesus (Lukas 17;11–19).

8 Die Herkunft des Volkes der Samariter wird mit der Eroberung Israels durch Assyrien in Verbindung gebracht (722 v.Chr.). Ein Teil der Bevölkerung des Königreichs wurde damals nach Mesopotamien gebracht und an ihrer Stelle wurde eine fremde Bevölkerung mit einer anderen Kultur und anderen Glaubensvorstellungen angesiedelt (2 Kön 17;24-41). Im Laufe der Zeit wurden sie integriert, und ihre Glaubensvorstellungen vermischten sich mit denen der Israeliten. Das führte zu einer Religion, die aus vielen Quellen schöpfte und ihr Zentrum oben auf dem Berg Garizim hatte. Die Unterschiede zwischen Juden und Samaritern sorgten für gegenseitige Abneigung (siehe Johannes 4;9; *Talmud Jerušalaim: Shekalim* 1.4.3; *Shevi'it* 6.1.16; 8.8.1).

Nebeneinanderstellung des Samariters mit Jesus führt viele Predigerinnen und Prediger dazu, dessen barmherzige Einstellung alsvöllige Hingabe zu überhöhen. Es gilt jedoch zu beachten, dass der Epilog des Gleichnisses ein anderes Bild ergibt. Der Samariter nimmt am Ende seine Alltagstätigkeit wieder auf und lässt den Angegriffenen in der Obhut des Herbergsbesitzers zurück (10;35). Er ordnet nicht sein ganzes Leben dem Opfer des Raubüberfalls unter, sondern hilft dem Mann entsprechend dessen Bedürfnissen.

Welche Konsequenzen hat die Botschaft Jesus für Menschen christlichen Glaubens heute? Diese lassen sich in mehreren Punkten ausdrücken:

1. Sie werden vielleicht mit einer Situation konfrontiert, in der ein Nächster dringend Hilfe braucht.
2. Einer religiösen Institution anzugehören ist kein Garant für eine anständige Einstellung gegenüber Bedürftigen.
3. Handeln Sie ungeachtet der negativen Werturteile anderer nach dem, was gut und richtig ist.
4. Helfen Sie jedem Menschen in Not, selbst wenn das vorübergehend zu Lasten Ihrer eigenen Bequemlichkeit, Besitztümer oder Zeit geht.
5. Handeln Sie angemessen, um die Bedürfnisse Ihres Nächsten zu erfüllen.

Die moderne Welt lässt es nicht zu, dass wir dieses Gleichnis nur aus der Sicht eines einzelnen Mannes betrachten. Heutzutage sind ganze Staaten und selbst Kontinente in Mitleidenschaft gezogen, was eine systemische und globale Reaktion erforderlich macht. Um heutigen Opfern zu helfen, wurden zahlreiche religiöse und internationale Organisationen gegründet. Das massive Ungleichgewicht beim Reichtum und die enorme Ungleichheit in den Lebensstandards haben dazu geführt, dass Menschen auf der Suche nach besseren Lebensbedingungen in Wellen migrieren. Viele Flüchtlinge wurden durch eine Reihe von blutigen regionalen Konflikten aus ihrer Heimat vertrieben. Wohlhabende Länder und Regionen müssen deshalb bewusst Maßnahmen ergreifen, um das Elend der Opfer solcher verheerenden Phänomene zu lindern. In den vergangenen Jahrzehnten sahen wir Beispiele sowohl für heroische Freigiebigkeit ohnegleichen als auch für gefühllose Gleichgültigkeit. Deshalb müssen wir darum beten, dass die internationale Gemeinschaft aus ihren Fehlern lernt und effektiv zur Tat schreitet. Auch einzelnen Kirchen, vor allem denjenigen mit globaler Reichweite, kommt eine wichtige Rolle zu.

Dennoch sollte jeder und jede damit beginnen, sich selber zu fragen: Inwieweit bin ich für eine andere Person der oder die Nächste? Inwieweit verhalte ich mich wie ein Nächster? Das Gleichnis Jesu ist eine Art Aufruf, eine Aufforderung an uns, ein Nächster zu sein, selbst wenn das bedeutet, einen Teil unserer eigenen Bequemlichkeit, Besitztümer und Zeit zu opfern.

Jesus‘ Antwort auf die Frage des Schriftgelehrten lautet also de facto: „JEDER". Die Jünger Christi sind somit aufgerufen, religiöse, kulturelle und politische Schranken zu überwinden und Menschen in Not eine helfende Hand zu reichen. Das Thema dieser Vollversammlung, „Die Liebe Christi bewegt die Welt zur Versöhnung und Einheit", kann deshalb auch so ausgedrückt werden: „Die Barmherzigkeit Christi bringt uns dazu, unseren Nächsten in jedem Menschen zu entdecken."

DIE LIEBE CHRISTI—BARMHERZIGKEIT FÜR DAS LEBEN—BEJAHUNG DER GANZHEIT DES LEBENS

Diana Tsaghikyan

[1]Und Jesus ging vorüber und sah einen Menschen, der blind geboren war. [2]Und seine Jünger fragten ihn und sprachen: Rabbi, wer hat gesündigt, dieser oder seine Eltern, dass er blind geboren ist? [3]Jesus antwortete: Es hat weder dieser gesündigt noch seine Eltern, sondern es sollen die Werke Gottes offenbar werden an ihm. [4]Wir müssen die Werke dessen wirken, der mich gesandt hat, solange es Tag ist; es kommt die Nacht, da niemand wirken kann. [5]Solange ich in der Welt bin, bin ich das Licht der Welt. [6]Als er das gesagt hatte, spuckte er auf die Erde, machte daraus einen Brei und strich den Brei auf die Augen des Blinden [7]und sprach zu ihm: Geh zu dem Teich Siloah – das heißt übersetzt: gesandt – und wasche dich! Da ging er hin und wusch sich und kam sehend wieder. [8]Die Nachbarn nun und die, die ihn zuvor als Bettler gesehen hatten, sprachen: Ist das nicht der Mann, der dasaß und bettelte? [9]Einige sprachen: Er ist‘s; andere: Nein, aber er ist ihm ähnlich. Er selbst aber sprach: Ich bin‘s. [10]Da fragten sie ihn: Wie sind deine Augen aufgetan worden? [11]Er antwortete: Der Mensch, der Jesus heißt, machte einen Brei und strich ihn auf meine Augen und sprach: Geh zum Teich Siloah und wasche dich! Ich ging hin und wusch mich und wurde sehend. [12]Da fragten sie ihn: Wo ist er? Er sprach: Ich weiß es nicht.
—Johannes 9;1–12

Üblicherweise sehen die Menschen die Heilung des Blinden als ein Wunder. Jesus sah den Blinden und befähigte ihn auf wunderbare Weise zu sehen. Die Heilung des Blinden war tatsächlich ein Wunder. Wunder geschahen damals, und auch heute geschehen Wunder auf vielfältige Weise. Dennoch geht es in dieser Geschichte nicht nur um ein Wunder, sondern es geht auch um die Liebe Christi und die Macht der Barmherzigkeit.

Was wissen wir über den Bettler? Dieser Mann hatte Eltern, aber war allein. Er lebte in der Gesellschaft, war jedoch von ihr ausgeschlossen. Von Geburt an blind hatte er nie das Licht erblickt, bis Christus ihn sah und seine Wirklichkeit veränderte. Zuerst lesen wir, dass Jesus einen blinden Menschen sieht, und dann werden wir sogleich Zeuge, wie Jesus das Diktum „Lass keinen Blinden und Lahmen ins Haus!“ (2 Sam. 5;8) verwirft. Jesus korrigiert die irrige Meinung seiner Jünger über Sünde und Leiden, unterrichtet sie über die Werke Gottes und erleuchtet sie mit seiner Erklärung: „Solange ich in der Welt bin, bin ich das Licht der Welt.“ Dann stellt Jesus mit seinem Speichel einen Brei aus Schlamm her, streicht ihn auf die Augen des Mannes und spricht: „Geh zu dem Teich Siloah und wasche dich!“ Nachdem der Bettler diese Anweisungen befolgt hat, kehrt er zurück und kann wieder sehen.

Ein unglaubliches Wunder ist geschehen, doch scheint sich niemand für den ehemals Blinden zu freuen oder sich für ihn zu interessieren. Wir werden vielleicht Zeuge von Gleichgültigkeit anstelle der benötigten Fürsorge und Barmherzigkeit. Interessanterweise sehen wir unter den Fragen, die die anderen stellen, keine einzige, mit der versucht wird, seine Gefühle und neu entstandenen Eindrücke zu ergründen. Statt auf Fürsorge und Mitgefühl stößt er auf Gleichgültigkeit. Im Gegensatz dazu heilt Jesus einen Blinden, der ausgeschlossen und ausgegrenzt war, aus reiner Liebe und Gnade. Jesus fordert Gesellschaft und Taten heraus. Er schenkt dem Bettler ein tiefes Gefühl von Hoffnung und ein innigeres Bewusstsein von Gottes erlösender Macht. Für den Mann stellt er mit einem neuen Zweck und einer neuen Richtung die Ganzheit des Lebens wieder her. Jesus gibt dem Mann die Vision von Licht.

Enttäuschung, Verdrossenheit und ein Mangel an Lebensvision können unser gegenwärtiges Dasein und unsere zukünftigen Hoffnungen mit der Schwärze der Ungewissheit verdüstern, doch in Zeiten der Finsternis ist es lebenswichtig, an einer Vision des Lichts festzuhalten. Wir können nicht in der Höhle des Todes verbleiben, wo die Verstandeskraft zum Schweigen gebracht wurde und weder Frömmigkeit noch Barmherzigkeit zu finden sind. Heute mehr denn je—nach 2022 Jahren—stehen die Kirchen noch immer vor vielen Herausforderungen. Es bedarf einer kostbaren Medizin, um die Wunden am Leib Christi zu heilen. Barmherzigkeit muss die Antwort sein.

Wahre Barmherzigkeit hat eine besondere Bedeutung in der Art, wie wir andere behandeln. Sie hat die Macht, Menschen auf den rechten Pfad zu bringen, wo die Liebe Christi verdeutlicht wird und das Licht zu sehen ist. Wahre Barmherzigkeit verändert die Art, wie wir leben. Wenn wir Barmherzigkeit mit offenen Armen in unserem Leben umfangen, versuchen wir voll Mitgefühl, Hoffnung, Glaube und Geduld zu sein. In Zeiten der Ungeduld müssen wir uns ins Gedächtnis rufen, dass Gottes Wege unergründlich sind. Wir müssen wertschätzen, wie die Barmherzigkeit uns daran erinnert, was es heißt, Mensch zu sein.

Jeder Aspekt dieser Geschichte hat eine spirituelle Bedeutung. Sie weist eine gewaltige Parallele zur Rolle Gottes auf, die uns durch die Gnade und die Macht der Barmherzigkeit zum Glauben und zur Erlösung bringt. Barmherzigkeit ist eine grundlegende Eigenschaft der biblischen Vorstellung von Gott. Jesus Christus, in dem Gott ward „offenbart im Fleisch" (1 Tim. 3:16), ist ein herausragendes Beispiel für Barmherzigkeit. Jesus lehrte, dass Barmherzigkeit sich nicht nur auf Freunde und Nächste erstrecken darf, sondern ausnahmslos auf alle, auf die gesamte menschliche Rasse. Der Evangelist Johannes möchte uns wiederherstellen und unsere Vision vom Licht bewahren.

Jede Epoche hat ihre Gebote. In unserer materialistischen und weltlichen Zeit, in Anbetracht einer weltweiten Pandemie, wenn wir der furchtbaren Realität von Rassismus, Diskriminierung, Armut, Gewalt, politischer Unsicherheit, Kriegen und Klimawandel gegenüberstehen, dürfen wir nicht aufgeben. Wir müssen die spirituellen Aspekte unseres Lebens mehr denn je wertschätzen. Ein jeder von uns ist einzigartig—wir haben unterschiedliche Ansichten, Kulturen, Erfahrungen und kommen aus unterschiedlichen Verhältnissen—doch unser gemeinsamer Glaube an Christus und unsere Liebe zum Herrn vereinen uns. Vor allem gibt es eine Einheit im Dienst und im Zeugnis überall auf der Welt im Namen von Jesus Christus, der „das Licht der Welt" ist. Ohne eine lebendige Beziehung mit unserem Schöpfer und miteinander fühlt sich das Leben hoffnungslos an. Jesus Christus öffnet den liebevollen Weg des gesegneten Lebens und dieser helle, lebensspendende Weg macht uns stark und gibt uns die Zuversicht, dass ein jeder von uns einen Lebens- und Schöpfungszweck hat.

Unser Herr Jesus Christus gab der Menschheit die Hoffnung und die Gnade, dem Leiden zu begegnen und das ewige Leben zu besitzen.

Ich glaube, dass wir mit gegenseitiger Achtung und dem festen Glauben an die Auferstehung Christi Gottes Wort verbreiten werden. Wir werden weiter demütig nach dem Licht Gottes streben und auf Versöhnung und Einheit hinarbeiten. Wir werden unseren persönlichen Zweck in Ehren halten, und mit dem von uns gefundenen Zweck werden wir auch der vielfältigen Menschheit unübersehbar Achtung erweisen. Zusammen mit diesem Zweck geht die Verantwortung einher, mit Barmherzigkeit, mit der Liebe Christi in Geist und Seele und geleitet von seinem unerschütterlichen Licht zu handeln. Jedoch können wir keine dieser Taten alleine vollbringen: wir brauchen einander. Gemeinsam können wir unserer Vergangenheit gedenken, unsere Gegenwart leben und unsere Zukunft gestalten. Wir wollen zusammen sein—ist das nicht ein Wunder?

> „Licht und Quelle der Erleuchtung,
> die da wohnen im unnahbaren
> Licht. . ..
> Bringe mit dem Anbruch des Tag-
> eslichts auch das Licht der Erkennt-
> nis in unsere Seelen.”[9]

9 Nerses Shnorhali (St. Nerses der Gnädige) war einer der bemerkenswertesten Theologen des Mittelalters und in der Geschichte der armenischen Kirche die ökumenische Figur schlechthin. Das obige Zitat stammt aus seinem „Hymnus an das Licht“ (Luys ararich Luso).

DIE LIEBE CHRISTI—VERWANDELNDE NACHFOLGE—BEJAHUNG VON GERECHTIGKEIT UND MENSCHENWÜRDE

Paulo Ueti

[21]Und Jesus ging weg von dort und entwich in die Gegend von Tyrus und Sidon. [22]Und siehe, eine kanaanäische Frau kam aus diesem Gebiet und schrie: Ach, Herr, du Sohn Davids, erbarme dich meiner! Meine Tochter wird von einem bösen Geist übel geplagt. [23]Er aber antwortete ihr kein Wort. Da traten seine Jünger zu ihm, baten ihn und sprachen: Lass sie doch gehen, denn sie schreit uns nach. [24]Er antwortete aber und sprach: Ich bin nur gesandt zu den verlorenen Schafen des Hauses Israel. [25]Sie aber kam und fiel vor ihm nieder und sprach: Herr, hilf mir! [26]Aber er antwortete und sprach: Es ist nicht recht, dass man den Kindern ihr Brot nehme und werfe es vor die Hunde. [27]Sie sprach: Ja, Herr; aber doch essen die Hunde von den Brosamen, die vom Tisch ihrer Herren fallen. [28]Da antwortete Jesus und sprach zu ihr: Frau, dein Glaube ist groß. Dir geschehe, wie du willst! Und ihre Tochter wurde gesund zu derselben Stunde.

—Matthäus 15:21–28

Matthäus‘ Version dieser Geschichte, mit mehr Elementen als die Version in Markus 7;24-30, ist sogar noch provokativer, denn hier erscheinen die Jünger Jesu in der Erzählung. Wir wissen, dass das Matthäus-Evangelium um 80-90 nach Chr. geschrieben wurde und sich nicht nur mit den Ereignissen während Jesus‘ Zeit in Palästina beschäftigte, sondern auch mit dem, was in der Kirche von Syrien geschah, der mutmaßlichen Quelle der meisten Schriften dieser Gemeinschaft.

In diesem Text geht es um Gemeinschaft. Es geht darum, wen wir aufnehmen und wie wir diese Person empfangen. Und als Text über eine Gemeinschaft stellt er eine Provokation dar in Sachen Willkommensbräuche, Versöhnung und Ausleben der Einheit in Jesus Christus. Unterschiedliche Menschen aus verschiedenen Kulturen, die sich in Sprache, Herkunft, Gebräuchen, Geschlecht, Alter und Stand unterscheiden, befinden sich in einem Kontext aus geschlechtsbezogener Gewalt, Rassismus, Bedürftigkeit, Schmerz, Krankheit, Ausgrenzung, Fremdenfeindlichkeit und bestehenden Vorurteile.

Wir müssen jedoch immer daran denken: Gott „hat den Fremdling lieb“ (Deut. 10;18). Wenn wir den Textkorpus im biblischen Kanon lesen, fällt uns auf, dass der Geist der Thora und der Propheten auch im Neuen Testament sehr präsent ist, wenn es darum geht sich für den Schutz von Menschen einzusetzen, die mit Unterdrückung, Krankheit, Ausgrenzung und Gewalt konfrontiert sind, die im System benachteiligt werden und die eine Art von Bedürftigkeit erleben, die dazu führt, dass sie als weniger menschlich wahrgenommen werden. Es sind die Armen, Fremde, Waisen, Witwen, Kinder und Frauen, die am meisten geschützt werden müssen.

Durch die Methodik des Dialogs entfaltet sich im Text die Begegnung einer fremdländischen Frau mit Jesus, dem Juden. Sie ist Kanaanäerin, von der Kultur her hellenistisch. Es scheint, dass ihr „Fremdsein" für den Verfasser dieser Geschichte relevant war. Für die Gemeinschaft scheint das Gespräch, die Beziehungen mit und die Aufnahme von Fremden, Ausländern und Frauen am Tisch des Herrn ein Problem zu sein. Wir wissen, dass ein gemeinsamer Tisch, *Koinonia*, stellvertretend für den Gottesdienst steht, für das Feiern und Erkennen von Jesus, der unter uns wandelt. Der gemeinsame Tisch heilt uns und bringt uns zusammen—oder sollte es tun.

Wir bemerken, dass dem Verfasser daran lag, die beiden—namenlosen—Frauen—die Tochter und die Mutter—in den Vordergrund zu rücken. Die Szene wird als eine zu Beginn wenig freundliche Begegnung zwischen zwei Menschen dargestellt, die normalerweise nicht einmal Blicke wechseln würden, geschweige denn miteinander reden. Für viele Menschen der damaligen Zeit waren Nicht-Juden „Hunde", so wie Nicht-Römer Barbaren waren. Dennoch fand das Zusammentreffen statt. Es gibt einen Wortwechsel, anscheinend zwischen Ungleichen, doch wenn wir das Gespräch analysieren, merken wir, dass sich die beiden auf der gleichen Stufe befinden, was die Bereitschaft, sich mit dem Gegenüber auseinanderzusetzen, die Gesprächstechnik und den Inhalt des Gesprächs angeht. Die Frau ist nicht völlig unterwürfig. Sie beteiligt sich, ist geschickt, belastbar und beharrlich, um zu kriegen, was sie möchte.

Das Gespräch entspinnt sich wegen der Krankheit der Tochter der Frau, wegen ihrer Erwartungen an Jesus und ihrer Kühnheit, Jesus zu stören, der im Verborgenen bleiben möchte. Die Frau bietet dem Mann die Stirn, der ihre Not nicht beachten will, und sie bekommt es mit Grobheiten und einem Mangel an Empathie von Seiten der Jünger zu tun. Laut dem Matthäus-Text schrie sie ihnen nach. Stellen Sie sich die unangenehme Szene vor, wie eine Frau jemandem nachschreit, der unerkannt bleiben möchte. Als sich die beiden gegenüberstehen, legt Jesus seine Position dar, die aus seiner kulturellen Tradition und dem herrührt, was er als Kind gelernt hat und mit dem er aufwuchs. Es widerstrebt ihm, das Brot und den Tisch zu teilen—eine Metapher für die Gemeinschaft, eine Unterstützergruppe. Es scheint, als bereite es der Gemeinschaft von Matthäus ein Problem, wer mit am Tisch sitzen darf.

Im weiteren Handlungsverlauf ist es interessant zu sehen, welche Themen den Dialog der beiden Menschen aus unterschiedlichen Kulturen durchziehen: eine Begegnung zwischen ungleichen Menschen; unreiner Geist/Notlage; Brot oben/Brosamen unten; auf dem Tisch/ unter dem Tisch. Es scheint, als sprächen sie über verschiedene Themen, die keinen Bezug zueinander haben. Die Frau, eine Griechin durch Bildung, hat ihre Bedürfnisse (Heilung ihrer Tochter, Austreibung eines bösen Geistes, sie will ihre Tochter zurück, Hilfe herbeiholen, sich selbst in das sprachliche Universum Jesu einschreiben). Jesus ist kulturell unnachgiebig (ethnozentrisch und intolerant), und er versucht, ihr den Zugang zum Tisch zu verweigern. Im Bericht des Matthäus haben wir noch die Jünger, die Jesus bitten: „Laß sie doch gehen" —was heißen kann, sie nicht zu „beachten" oder „sie wegzuschicken, ohne ihr Beistand zu leisten"— in beiden Fällen haben wir hier Mittelsmänner, die sich an dieser Beziehung stören. In der Gemeinschaft im Matthäus-Evangelium scheint es, als dürfe die Frau kein Recht auf Zugang zum Tisch, das heißt zu Jesus, haben.

Die grundlegende Frage der Frau, die sie mit Frömmigkeit und rhetorischem Geschick entwickelt, lautet: Wer hat Zugang zu Jesus? Wer kann zum Brot gelangen? Sind es nur die Kinder Israels, diejenigen im Club Jesu und die

Jünger; die, die vorbereitet sind; die, die frei von Sünde sind? Die beiden Texte zeigen, dass das die ersten Gedanken und Worte von Jesus waren. Die Frau akzeptierte diese kulturelle und gesellschaftliche Norm nicht. Sie mochte nicht in einer Welt leben, in der es Norm war, Menschen wie sie und ihresgleichen auszuschließen. Sie überschritt die einheitliche und dominierende Sprache dieser Kultur, Tradition und Religion und brachte diesen Mann dazu, seine Meinung und seine Haltung zu ändern. Sie schuf eine Einsicht, mit dem die Grundlage für eine neue erkenntnistheoretische Möglichkeit gelegt wurde: „Aus dem Munde der jungen Kinder und Säuglinge hast du eine Macht zugerichtet" (Ps. 8;2a).

Im literarischen Kontext ist es auch interessant, dass sich dieser Text zwischen zwei anderen befindet, in denen Brot erwähnt wird:

> Matthäus 14;13–21. Das erste Teilen der Brote mit 5000 Menschen; 12 Körbe voll blieben übrig.
> Matthäus 15;21–28. Unsere zwiespältige Geschichte darüber, wer Zugang zu Jesus/dem Brot/den Brosamen hat.
> Matthäus 15; 15;32–38. Das zweite Teilen der Brote mit 4000 Menschen; 7 Körbe voll blieben übrig.

Diese Korrelation finden wir sowohl bei Markus als auch bei Matthäus. Es scheint, dass die Geschichte der syrophönizischen Frau, die mit Jesus darüber debattiert, wer Zugang zum Brot haben oder Heilung bekommen könne, dazu führen musste, dass die erste Geschichte von der Vermehrung der Brote noch einmal erzählt wurde und ein anderes Ende erhielt, um zu bekräftigen, dass alle Menschen Zugang zu Jesus haben. An dieser Stelle sollten wir uns daran erinnern, dass Zugang zu Jesus auch Zugang zur Gemeinschaft, zu einem neuen Projekt und zum politischen und ideotheolgischen Raum bedeutet, was gegen alles verstößt, was damals und auch heute etabliert war und ist.

Alle haben Zugang zu Jesus/zum Tisch/zur Kommunion/zur Gemeinschaft/zum Dialog

> Hier ist nicht Jude noch Grieche, hier ist nicht Sklave noch Freier,
> hier ist nicht Mann noch Frau; denn ihr seid allesamt einer in Christus Jesus.
>
> **—Galater 3;28**

Zugang zu Jesus, zum Brot oder den Brosamen, die vom Tisch fallen, hängt mit dem Aufeinandertreffen und den Diskrepanzen zwischen Menschen aus unterschiedlichen Kulturen zusammen, die einen unterschiedlichen Wortschatz und jeweils andere Bedürfnisse und Wünsche haben, etwas voneinander zu lernen. Darum legt unsere Episode so viel Wert auf die Kultur und geographische Lage der beiden Figuren und ihre Bedürfnisse: die Frau und ihre Tochter, denen es an Beziehungen und Teilhabe mangelt—Brot, Tisch, Gesundheit, Gemeinschaft, Unterstützung, Anerkennung—und Jesus und seine engsten Jünger (alles Männer, wohlgemerkt), die im kulturellen Ethnozentrismus gefangen sind, der Fremdenfeindlichkeit und Gewalt hervorruft. Trotzdem wurden diese Männer mit der Fähigkeit gesegnet, zuzuhören und selbst bei Meinungsverschiedenheiten ihre vermeintliche Überlegenheit zu überwinden und bis zum Schluss im Dialog zu bleiben. Es scheint, als könnten Gesundheit und Leben nur in einem dialogischen Prozess auftreten. Hierin mag eine Warnung an die Gemeinschaft enthalten sein, dass Offenheit für neue Beziehungen, spirituelles und professionelles Zuhören, Solidarität, ein Gefühl von Gleichheit und ein Austausch erforderlich sind, um

Meinungsverschiedenheiten in Begegnungen der Liebe und des Lebens zu verwandeln. Solche Begegnungen verhindern Krankheit und Tod und verwandeln uns. Im 1. Brief an die Korinther 11;28-32 verurteilte Paulus die Praxis des Abendmahls in der korinthischen Gemeinschaft, nämlich zu essen ohne sich vorher selbst zu prüfen. Auch heute gibt es viele Schwache und Kranke und nicht wenige sind entschlafen, denn die Gemeinschaft war nicht unterstützend—darum die Ermahnung, sich selbst zu prüfen, um sich nicht selbst zu verdammen.

Wir müssen wieder „verlernen". „[...] was töricht ist vor der Welt, das hat Gott erwählt, [auch] das, was nichts ist, damit er zunichtemache, was etwas ist" (1. Kor. 1;27-28). Jesus bzw. die Gemeinschaft verlernte etwas, um mehr zu begreifen. Dieses Resultat wird durch die Begegnungen zwischen verschiedenen Kulturen hervorgerufen, wenn wir wahrhaft offen und bereit sind, uns in die Richtung zu bewegen, in der wir uns selbst von unseren Wahrheiten, Traditionen und Gewissheiten loslösen. Auf diese Weise können wir unsere Aufmerksamkeit auf den wesentlichen Standpunkt unserer Befreiungsspiritualität richten: nämlich auf den Gott zu hören, der uns Leben schenkt und in einer pluralistischen und vielfältigen Welt zu uns kommt, und Ihm zu gehorchen.

Die Frau lässt sich von dem Problem, dass ihr keine Beachtung geschenkt wird, nicht entmutigen. Sie ist ein Opfer, doch sie ist nicht passiv. Sie hat Rechte und dessen ist sie sich bewusst. Das verleiht ihr die Kraft (dynamo) vorzurücken (entgegenzutreten). Selbst aus ihrer Stellung als „Hund" (wie sie faktisch behauptet) heraus bekräftigt sie, dass dies kein Problem sei, das sie von der vollen Teilhabe an der Gemeinschaft abhalten kann.

Diese Erzählung steht meiner Meinung nach in einer Reihe mit anderen, in denen betont wird, dass unsere Mentalität, unsere Theologien, unsere Bräuche und unsere pastorale Fürsorge antirassistisch, antifremdenfeindlich und gegen jede Art von Gewalt sein müssen. Ebenso fordert sie uns auf, bedingungslos all jenen Beistand zu leisten, die Hilfe benötigen und auf die Konflikte zu achten, die daraus in der kirchlichen Gemeinschaft und auch in unserem gemeinsamen Heim, der *Oikoumene* und dem Planeten, entstehen können. Suchen wir den Dialog und bleiben wir im Dialog, selbst wenn wir gekränkt, ausgeschlossen und in unserer Menschlichkeit herabgesetzt werden? Wie können wir daraus eine Praxis entwickeln, die sich auf die Umgebung und den Kontext, in denen wir leben, erstreckt?

Hinauszugehen, um andere zu treffen, stellt immer eine Herausforderung dar. Doch das ist unsere Berufung. Hören wir, wie der Sämann im Gleichnis[10], den Ruf zu säen, egal wie schwierig der Boden ist?

Möge uns die Dreifaltigkeit mit dem für unsere Spiritualität so bezeichnenden Geist der Entrüstung und Widerstandskraft segnen.

Die Einheit der Kirche, sagt Jesus, kann durch die Umkehr solcher Machtkonzepte hochgehalten und neubelebt werden, indem diese durch die Macht des Dienstes (*Diakonia*) ersetzt werden. Dieser Dienst ist wahrhaft einend, wenn er die Handlungsfähigkeit der Menschen auf der Empfängerseite nicht außer Kraft setzt oder ersetzt. *Diakonia*, die der Einheit der Kirche dient, wird in Liebe, in aufopfernder Liebe, erbracht. Diese Liebe muss größer sein als die mütterliche Liebe für zwei Söhne. Mit genau dieser Liebe liebte Gott die ganze Menschheit. Es ist eine Liebe, die zwar über väterliche und mütterliche Bündnisse hinausgeht, aber neue

10 Matthäus 13;3–8; Markus 4;3–8; Lukas 8;5–8.

Zusammenschlüsse aus der Liebe von Brüdern und Schwestern in Gottes Familie bildet. Es ist eine Liebe, die über ideologische Bündnisse hinausgeht, die dazu dienen, die exklusiven Privilegien einiger Weniger zu bewahren. Diese wahre Liebe macht den Kreis größer, um all die Menschen aufzunehmen, die normalerweise davon ausgeschlossen wären. Eine solche Liebe reißt die Mauern von Rasse und ethnischem Fanatismus und Stolz nieder. Diese Liebe mach einen demütig, ohne zu erniedrigen.

Diese Liebe wird im selbst-aufopferndem Dienst eines Knechts, dem *Doulos*, in Demut ausgedrückt. Die Liebe, die diese Art von Dienst annimmt, basiert nicht auf erotischen und leidenschaftlichen Gefühlen. Sie ist kein bloßer kindlicher Respekt oder basiert rein auf Freundschaft. Sie begründet sich nicht zwangsläufig auf der elterlichen Liebe zu ihren Kindern oder der Liebe zu Freunden und Verwandten. Ihr sprudelnder Quell muss die Agape sein, die Liebe all jener, die als Ebenbild Gottes erschaffen wurden. Das ist die Liebe, die Gott mit uns in Jesus Christus geteilt hat. Diese Liebe ist es, die das Gift der unterdrückenden Formen von Macht in der Kirche und auf der Welt beseitigen kann.

Die von dieser Liebe angetriebene Kirche ist ein mächtiges Zeugnis in der Welt, denn sie bietet eine Alternative zur Machtausübung. Die kirchliche Machtausübung darf kein Abbild der weltlichen Machtausübung sein. Sie muss das Salz und das Licht der Welt sein. Durch das Zeugnis ihrer Mitglieder, die als Stellvertretende des nahenden Reichs Gottes in der Gesellschaft leben, trägt die Kirche zur Verwandlung der verzerrten Machtverteilung auf der Welt bei. Durch ihr vorbildliches Leben und ihre Worte, in ihren Familien, in ihren Gemeinden, in der Kirche und im öffentlichen Raum bestehen sie gegen die Pforten des Hades.

Auch legt die Kirche vor der Welt Zeugnis ab, wenn sie uneingeschränkt Stellungen bezieht, die zuweilen unpopulär und unsicher sind. Jesus spricht: „Eure Rede aber sei: Ja, ja; nein, nein. Was darüber ist, das ist vom Bösen“ (Matthäus 5;37). Das mutige und aufopfernde Zeugnis der Kirche zielt darauf ab, sich allen Systemen, die ungerechte und ungleiche Machtverhältnisse in der Welt und in der Kirche schaffen, zu widersetzen, sie zu schwächen und schließlich mit den Wurzeln auszureißen. Glaubensgetreue Kirchen müssen sagen können: „So soll es bei uns nicht sein!“ Das sollen Kirchen auf lokaler, regionaler, nationaler und globaler Ebene sagen. Die Kirche soll „Nein“ sagen zu zunehmendem Militarismus, unproduktiven Märkten, Materialismus, Monokulturismus, Manipulation, Falschinformation, Böswilligkeit, Lynchjustiz und zu wachsenden Monopolstellungen über die Öffentlichkeit und die Masse des Volkes. Genauso soll die Kirche ein nachdrückliches „JA!“ rufen. Ja zu Mitleid und Barmherzigkeit, zu bedeutungsvollen Beziehungen, zu multilateraler Zusammenarbeit der Nationen, zur Vermittlung in Konflikten, zur Mäßigung in Ämtern und zur Gegenseitigkeit. Das ist die Neuverteilung von Macht, zu der uns Jesus auffordert!

DIE LIEBE CHRISTI—DAS BAND DER CHRISTLICHEN EINHEIT UND DAS GEMEINSAME ZEUGNIS DER KIRCHEN

Kenneth Mtata

[20]Da trat zu ihm die Mutter der Söhne des Zebedäus mit ihren Söhnen, fiel vor ihm nieder und wollte ihn um etwas bitten. [21]Und er sprach zu ihr: Was willst du? Sie sprach zu ihm: Lass diese meine beiden Söhne sitzen in deinem Reich, einen zu deiner Rechten und den andern zu deiner Linken. [22]Aber Jesus antwortete und sprach: Ihr wisst nicht, was ihr bittet. Könnt ihr den Kelch trinken, den ich trinken werde? Sie sprachen zu ihm: Ja, das können wir. [23]Er sprach zu ihnen: Meinen Kelch werdet ihr zwar trinken, aber das Sitzen zu meiner Rechten und Linken zu geben steht mir nicht zu. Das wird denen zuteil, für die es bestimmt ist von meinem Vater. [24]Als das die Zehn hörten, wurden sie unwillig über die zwei Brüder. [25]Aber Jesus rief sie zu sich und sprach: Ihr wisst, dass die Herrscher ihre Völker niederhalten und die Mächtigen ihnen Gewalt antun. [26]So soll es nicht sein unter euch; sondern wer unter euch groß sein will, der sei euer Diener; [27]und wer unter euch der Erste sein will, der sei euer Knecht, [28]so wie der Menschensohn nicht gekommen ist, dass er sich dienen lasse, sondern dass er diene und gebe sein Leben als Lösegeld für viele.

—Matthäus 20;20–28

Die Mutter der beiden Söhne des Zebedäus tritt in einer unterwürfigen Haltung, die schon an Anbetung (προσκυνοῦσα) grenzt, an Jesus heran, um ihn um eine Gunst für ihre beiden Söhne zu bitten. Obwohl die beiden Söhne unter dem Namen ihres Vaters Zebedäus bekannt sind, nutzt sie ihre mütterliche Autorität, um deren Erhöhung zu erflehen. Das ist typisch für traditionsgebundene Kulturen, in denen die Herrschaft klar von den Vätern ausgeübt wird, während außerhalb der Sicht der Öffentlichkeit die wahre Macht bei den Müttern liegt. Jedenfalls strebt sie für ihre Söhne nach dem, was das Matthäus-Evangelium als höchstes Ziel darstellt: „Trachtet zuerst nach dem Reich Gottes und nach seiner Gerechtigkeit, so wird euch das alles zufallen" (6;33).

Was durchdringt ihr Verständnis vom „Reich Gottes"? Einige Gelehrte lesen Matthäus' Verweis auf das Reich Gottes gerne vor dem Hintergrund, dass die „jüdisch-christliche Gemeinschaft dabei war, ihre eigene Identität noch einmal neu zu definieren, um sich von der jüdischen Gegenseite abzugrenzen, die sich zu der Zeit unter der Führung pharisäischer Schriftgelehrter verfestigte."[11] Andere sehen das gesamte Matthäus-Evangelium im Allgemeinen und den Sprachgebrauch vom Reich Gottes im Speziellen im größeren Zusammenhang mit der Macht und Herrschaft des römischen Imperiums.[12] Die beiden Schwerpunkte schließen sich nicht unbedingt gegenseitig aus. Es ist

11 A. B. Du Toit, „The Kingdom of God in the Gospel of Matthew", *Skrif en Kerk* 21, Nr. 3 (2000), 545.

12 Boris Repschinsk, „Kingdoms of the Earth and the Kingdom of the Heavens: Matthew's Perspective on Political Power", in *The Composition, Theology, and Early Reception of Matthew's Gospel*, Hrsg. Joseph Verheyden, Jens Schröter und David C. Sim (Tübingen: Mohr Siebeck, 2022), 149.

bekannt, dass die Römer mit ihrer geballten Anwesenheit in Antiochia das gesellschaftliche Umfeld der Gemeinschaften hinter dem Matthäus-Evangelium prägten. Diese Römer waren die „Heiden", die einem sofort einfallen. Ihre Herrschaft über die von ihnen kolonisierten Untertanen übten sie mithilfe einer fügsamen und politischen Stellvertreterverwaltung aus, aber auch durch militärische Präsenz und religiöse Dominanz. In dieser Hinsicht übten die Römer tatsächliche „Macht über" (κατακυριεύουσιν) ihre Untertanen aus. Und wie alle kolonisierten Menschen wurden die Jünger und ihre Glaubensgemeinschaften von den Machtexzessen, die ihnen die unterdrückenden Römer vorführten, angezogen und ahmten diese nach. Daher ist es nicht überraschend, dass sie versuchten, ihre eigenen kleinen Reiche zu schaffen, die durch eine beherrschende „Macht über" und tyrannische Beziehungen gekennzeichnet waren. Vor diesem Hintergrund strebt die Mutter der Söhne des Zebedäus nach den besten Positionen für ihre Söhne. Dabei hofft sie auch, sich selbst einen besonderen Platz im Himmelreich zu sichern.

In Matthäus 20 zeigt Jesus jedoch einen neuen Entwurf von Macht als Macht im aufopfernden und demütigen Dienst (Verse 26–27). In einem solchen Denkmodell lässt sich das Reich Gottes am besten begreifen—wo Größe darin besteht, Diener (διάκονος) und sogar Knecht (δοῦλος) zu sein, wo ein solcher Dienst bis zum Tode dauern konnte. Im unmittelbaren Textzusammenhang des heutigen Abschnitts sagt Jesus seinen Tod voraus (Verse 17–19) und heilt zwei Blinde (als Gegensatz zu den beiden Söhnen des Zebedäus?) als er aus Jericho hinauszieht (Verse 29–34). Es ist der Tod Jesu, der uns die Augen für wahre Größe öffnet. Jesus ist nicht nur der Lehrmeister, sondern auch das vollendete Beispiel für *Diakonia* oder demütigen Dienst.

Was bedeutet das für uns?

„Als das die Zehn hörten, wurden sie unwillig über die zwei Brüder" (V. 24). Mary Jane Gorman sagt: „Wir können uns mit der Entrüstung der zehn anderen Jünger identifizieren: Wenn wir tugendhaft widerstanden und nicht um den Platz neben dem Ehrengast gebeten haben, dann wären wir vermutlich auch verärgert, wenn jemand anderes fragt, ob er dort sitzen darf."[13] So wie die Einheit der Jünger durch diesen Akt selbstsüchtiger Macht bedroht wurde, so leidet auch die Kirche unter der Last tyrannischer, kontrollsüchtiger und privilegierter Macht, da diese wiederum eine Reaktion der Entrüstung, der Missgunst und des Misstrauens erzeugt.

Genau wie im Kontext des römischen Reichs scheint die Welt heute von militaristischen, exklusivistischen, götzendienerischen Formen der Macht befrachtet zu sein. Dieser Ausdruck unterdrückender Macht kann durch eine trügerische Vaterherrschaft und mütterliche Bündnisse (eine Mutter, die ihren Söhnen einen besonderen Platz besorgt), absolutistische links- und rechtsextreme Ideologien (der eine zur Rechten und der andere zur Linken) oder Vetternwirtschaft aufgrund von ethnischer Zugehörigkeit und Identität (Söhne des Zebedäus) aufrechterhalten werden – und das alles unter dem Deckmantel von Religiosität und Frömmigkeit (Streben nach dem Reich Gottes).

Die Einheit der Kirche, sagt Jesus, kann durch die Umkehr solcher Machtkonzepte hochgehalten und neubelebt werden, indem diese durch die Macht des Dienstes (*Diakonia*) ersetzt werden.

13 Mary Jane Gorman, *Watching the Disciples: Learning from Their Mistakes*, (Nashville, TN: Abingdon Press, 2008), https://books.google.co.za/books?id=-ax0qIW55nkC&pg.

Dieser Dienst ist wahrhaft einend, wenn er die Handlungsfähigkeit der Menschen auf der Empfängerseite nicht außer Kraft setzt oder ersetzt. *Diakonia*, die der Einheit der Kirche dient, wird in Liebe, in aufopfernder Liebe, erbracht. Diese Liebe muss größer sein als die mütterliche Liebe für zwei Söhne. Mit genau dieser Liebe liebte Gott die ganze Menschheit. Es ist eine Liebe, die zwar über väterliche und mütterliche Bündnisse hinausgeht, aber neue Zusammenschlüsse aus der Liebe von Brüdern und Schwestern in Gottes Familie bildet. Es ist eine Liebe, die über ideologische Bündnisse hinausgeht, die dazu dienen, die exklusiven Privilegien einiger Weniger zu bewahren. Diese wahre Liebe macht den Kreis größer, um all die Menschen aufzunehmen, die normalerweise davon ausgeschlossen wären. Eine solche Liebe reißt die Mauern von Rasse und ethnischem Fanatismus und Stolz nieder. Diese Liebe mach einen demütig, ohne zu erniedrigen.

Diese Liebe wird im selbst-aufopferndem Dienst eines Knechts, dem *Doulos*, in Demut ausgedrückt. Die Liebe, die diese Art von Dienst annimmt, basiert nicht auf erotischen und leidenschaftlichen Gefühlen. Sie ist kein bloßer kindlicher Respekt oder basiert rein auf Freundschaft. Sie begründet sich nicht zwangsläufig auf der elterlichen Liebe zu ihren Kindern oder der Liebe zu Freunden und Verwandten. Ihr sprudelnder Quell muss die Agape sein, die Liebe all jener, die als Ebenbild Gottes erschaffen wurden. Das ist die Liebe, die Gott mit uns in Jesus Christus geteilt hat. Diese Liebe ist es, die das Gift der unterdrückenden Formen von Macht in der Kirche und auf der Welt beseitigen kann.

Die von dieser Liebe angetriebene Kirche ist ein mächtiges Zeugnis in der Welt, denn sie bietet eine Alternative zur Machtausübung. Die kirchliche Machtausübung darf kein Abbild der weltlichen Machtausübung sein. Sie muss das Salz und das Licht der Welt sein. Durch das Zeugnis ihrer Mitglieder, die als Stellvertretende des nahenden Reichs Gottes in der Gesellschaft leben, trägt die Kirche zur Verwandlung der verzerrten Machtverteilung auf der Welt bei. Durch ihr vorbildliches Leben und ihre Worte, in ihren Familien, in ihren Gemeinden, in der Kirche und im öffentlichen Raum bestehen sie gegen die Pforten des Hades.

Auch legt die Kirche vor der Welt Zeugnis ab, wenn sie uneingeschränkt Stellungen bezieht, die zuweilen unpopulär und unsicher sind. Jesus spricht: „Eure Rede aber sei: Ja, ja; nein, nein. Was darüber ist, das ist vom Bösen“ (Matthäus 5;37). Das mutige und aufopfernde Zeugnis der Kirche zielt darauf ab, sich allen Systemen, die ungerechte und ungleiche Machtverhältnisse in der Welt und in der Kirche schaffen, zu widersetzen, sie zu schwächen und schließlich mit den Wurzeln auszureißen. Glaubensgetreue Kirchen müssen sagen können: „So soll es bei uns nicht sein!“ Das sollen Kirchen auf lokaler, regionaler, nationaler und globaler Ebene sagen. Die Kirche soll „Nein“ sagen zu zunehmendem Militarismus, unproduktiven Märkten, Materialismus, Monokulturismus, Manipulation, Falschinformation, Böswilligkeit, Lynchjustiz und zu wachsenden Monopolstellungen über die Öffentlichkeit und die Masse des Volkes. Genauso soll die Kirche ein nachdrückliches „JA!“ rufen. Ja zu Mitleid und Barmherzigkeit, zu bedeutungsvollen Beziehungen, zu multilateraler Zusammenarbeit der Nationen, zur Vermittlung in Konflikten, zur Mäßigung in Ämtern und zur Gegenseitigkeit. Das ist die Neuverteilung von Macht, zu der uns Jesus auffordert!

BEITRAGENDE

Pfarrerin Dr. **Hyunju Bae** ist ehemalige Professorin der Presbyterianischen Universität Busan in der Republik Korea und ordinierte Geistliche der presbyterianischen Kirche von Korea. Im Zeitraum zwischen den Vollversammlungen von Busan bis Karlsruhe war sie Mitglied im Exekutiv- und im Zentralausschuss des Ökumenischen Rats der Kirchen. Sie ist Co-Präsidentin der christlichen Umweltschutzbewegung Koreas Solidarität für die Unversehrtheit der Schöpfung.

Archimandrit Prof. Dr. **Jack Khalil** vom Griechisch-Orthodoxen Patriarchat von Antiochien und dem ganzen Osten ist Dekan des Theologischen Instituts des Hl. Johannes von Damaskus an der Universität von Balamand und Professor für neutestamentliche Studien. Er promovierte an der Aristotles-Universität von Thessaloniki und studierte drei Jahre als Gaststipendiat an der Eberhard-Karls-Universität in Tübingen, Deutschland. Außerdem ist er Mitglied des ÖRK Zentralausschusses und gehört der Kommission für Glauben und Kirchenverfassung an.

Dr. **Krzysztof Mielcarek** ist Theologe, Bibelwissenschaftler und Lehrbeauftragter an der Fakultät für Theologie in der Johannes Paul II. Katholischen Theologie von Lublin (Polen). Er ist einer der Herausgeber und Übersetzer der polnischen Ökumenischen Bibel (2017). Seit 2014 ist er römisch-katholisches Kommissionsmitglied in der Kommission für Glauben und Kirchenverfassung des Ökumenischen Rats der Kirchen.

Pfarrer Dr. **Kenneth Mtata** ist ein Theologe aus Simbabwe und Generalsekretär des Kirchenrats von Simbabwe. In seiner Arbeit befasst er sich mit Hermeneutik, der Kirche im öffentlichen Engagement und der Schnittstelle von Religion und sozialem Wandel. Er promovierte an der Universität von KsaZulu-Natal über Raum und Ort im Evangelium nach Johannes.

Dr. **Diana Tsaghikyan** ist Hochschulassistentin an der Fakultät für Theologie, Staatliche Universität von Jerewan, und Leiterin des Bachelor-Studienprogramms. Außerdem ist sie Mitglied im Komitee für Doktorarbeiten am Theologischen Seminar Geworkian (Universität), Heiliger Stuhl von St. Etschmiadsin. 2019 trat Dr. Tsaghikyan dem ÖRK als Vertreterin der Armenischen Apostolischen Kirche (Heiliger Stuhl von St. Etschmiadsin) und Mitglied des Zentralausschusses bei. Sie promovierte an der Universität Edinburgh und erwarb dort einen Master in Theologie (MTh). Außerdem erwarb sie einen Master in Religionswissenschaften am Zentralen Baptistischen Theologieseminar in KS, USA, und einen Bachelor an der Staatlichen Universität für Sprachen und Sozialwissenschaften in Jerewan. Dr. Tsaghikyans Forschungsschwerpunkt liegt auf patristischen Studien und christlicher Lehre. Ihr besonderes Interesse gilt der theologischen Literatur der armenischen Kirchenväter. Zu ihren weiteren Forschungsinteressen gehören ökumenische Studien und zeitgenössische Themen der Theologie.

Dr. **Paulo Ueti** ist Brasilianer mit japanischer Mutter und italienischem Vater. Er studiert lateinamerikanische Theologien, kontextuelle Bibelforschung, den Kanon des Neuen Testaments und dessen Beziehung zur Kirchengeschichte und Reichstheologie, Spiritualität, Gender,

Umweltgerechtigkeit und Ekklesiologie. Er ist Mitglied des Ökumenischen Zentrums für Bibelforschung (CEBI) der Anglikanischen Episkopalkirche von Brasilien und arbeitet in London im Büro der Anglikanischen Kirchengemeinschaft bei Anglican Alliance (Entwicklung, Nothilfe und Fürsprache) sowie im Referat für theologische Ausbildung.

TABLE DES MATIÈRES

INTRODUCTION

Les études bibliques en séance plénières thématiques constituent un aspect important des travaux de l'Assemblée. Elles sont pour les participant-e-s l'occasion de se réunir quotidiennement autour d'un passage de la Bible pour réfléchir sur le thème et l'expérience de l'Assemblée. Les participant-e-s peuvent discerner ensemble les desseins de Dieu pour elles ou eux et pour le mouvement œcuménique. Ils ou elles se réunissent en groupes suffisamment restreints pour permettre à tout le monde de contribuer, et suffisamment importants pour offrir un éventail de points de vue.
Les séances d'étude biblique permettent aux participant-e-s d'explorer le thème de l'Assemblée ensemble à la lumière des textes bibliques, des connaissances et des expériences. La participation à une étude biblique en groupe signifie l'ouverture aux autres, au passage de la Bible et au Saint- Esprit. Il ne s'agit pas de convaincre lors d'un débat ni de persuader les autres d'un point de vue donné. Ces séances doivent être un lieu où les participant-e-s peuvent intégrer tout ce qu'ils ou elles ont entendu ou fait lors de l'Assemblée et découvrir ensemble les possibilités de transformation que Dieu nous offre.

PRÉSENTATION

2e jour, jeudi 1er septembre 2022

Thème du jour: *Le dessein de l'amour de Dieu dans le Christ pour toute la création: réconciliation et unité*
Référence biblique: Col 1,19 f. (Ep 1,10) et Mt 9,35 f. (compassion du Christ)
Thème en séance plénière: *Le dessein de l'amour de Dieu incarné dans Jésus-Christ: réconciliation et unité*
Réflexion par: le père Jack Khalil et la pasteure Hyunju Bae

3e jour, vendredi 2 septembre 2022

Thème du jour: *L'Europe*
Référence biblique: Luc 10,25-37 (le Bon Samaritain)
Thème en séance plénière: *L'Europe*
Réflexion par: Krzysztof Mielcarek (Pologne/Europe)

6e jour, lundi 5 septembre 2022

Thème du jour: *L'amour du Christ: compassion pour la vie*
Référence biblique: Jean 9,1-12
Thème en séance plénière: *Affirmer la plénitude de la vie*
Réflexion par: Diana Tsaghikyan (Europe)

7e jour, mardi 6 septembre 2022

Thème du jour: *L'amour du Christ: transformer l'obéissance au Christ*
Référence biblique: Matthieu 15,21-28 (la Cananéenne)
Thème en séance plénière: *Affirmer la justice et la dignité humaine*
Réflexion par: Paulo Ueti (Brésil/Amérique du Sud)

8e jour, mercredi 7 septembre 2022

Thème du jour: *L'amour du Christ: le lien de l'unité chrétienne et le témoignage commun des Églises*
Référence biblique: Matthieu 20,20-28
Thème en plénières thématiques: *L'unité chrétienne et le témoignage commun des Églises*
Réflexion par: le pasteur Kenneth Mtata (Zimbabwe/Afrique)

Prions les uns pour les autres alors que nous nous préparons à effectuer cette tâche et à participer à l'Assemblée. Que l'amour du Christ mène le monde à la réconciliation et à l'unité.

LE DESSEIN DE L'AMOUR DE DIEU DANS LE CHRIST POUR TOUTE LA CRÉATION: RÉCONCILIATION ET UNITÉ

Jack Khalil

19 Car il a plu à Dieu de faire habiter en lui toute la plénitude, 20 et de tout réconcilier par lui et pour lui, et sur la terre et dans les cieux, ayant établi la paix par le sang de sa croix.
—Colossiens 1,19-20

Ces versets figurent dans le cantique christologique (Colossiens 1,15-20). Que ce passage provienne d'un cantique traditionnel plus ancien ou soit écrit par Saint Paul lui-même dans le style d'un cantique, il sonne comme une musique à l'oreille de celles et ceux qui aiment Dieu. Il associe l'économie divine du salut à la théologie de la création en identifiant le Rédempteur du monde au Créateur qui a tout fait naître. La première strophe (v. 15-18a) révèle l'identité du Christ en tant que créateur de toutes choses «dans les cieux et sur la terre» (v. 16), et se termine par un glissement sur le fait qu'il est le chef de l'Église (v. 18a). La deuxième strophe (v. 18b-20) expose la bienfaisance du Christ à l'égard de toute la création «sur la terre et dans les cieux» (v. 20), comme en témoignent son incarnation (v. 19), sa passion, sa mort et sa résurrection pour tous les humains. Il est clairement démontré que les événements historiques, abordés dans la deuxième strophe, sont étroitement liés à ce que la première strophe affirme: à savoir, que le Christ est le créateur de toutes choses; l'amour du Christ, manifesté en réconciliant toutes choses avec lui-même par son sang, s'enracine dans son amour manifesté lors de la création de toutes choses. La répétition de l'expression «toutes choses... dans les cieux et sur la terre» — tant dans la première strophe qui parle de leur création que dans la deuxième qui porte sur leur réconciliation — valide le commentaire précédent selon lequel la réconciliation de toutes choses vient de l'amour du Christ pour toutes les choses qu'Il a créées. L'amour du Christ va d'éternité en éternité. Celui-ci prend soin de toutes les choses sur la Terre comme au ciel et les garde, car elles Lui appartiennent.

L'amour du Christ nous appelle et nous mène à la réconciliation. Il nous appelle à nous repentir de notre hostilité envers Lui (v. 21), qui se manifeste en faisant du mal à notre prochain et à Son univers. Nous devons être conscient que notre péché envers Dieu ne se réduit pas au blasphème et à l'ingratitude; il s'agit plutôt d'un péché essentiellement lié aux relations humaines et à l'écologie.

Selon Romains 8,5, l'hostilité est une conséquence d'être «[s]ous l'empire de la chair», ce qui signifie s'efforcer de satisfaire le moi et les désirs égoïstes (Gal. 5,16) au détriment de nos co-humains. «[I]dolâtrie, magie, haines, discorde, jalousie, emportements, rivalités, dissensions, factions» (Ga 5,20) en sont les conséquences. En effet, les œuvres de la chair sont des exemples représentatifs des péchés relationnels. En ce sens, Colossiens 1,21 affirme que l'hostilité des humains envers Dieu existe en raison d'œuvres mauvaises.

Le fait que le péché et les œuvres mauvaises transforment les êtres humains en ennemis de Dieu ne signifie pas que le péché entraîne une hostilité mutuelle entre Dieu et les hommes ni que Dieu est hostile aux pécheurs. Un tel point de vue n'apparaît nulle part dans les épîtres de Saint-Paul. Au contraire, Paul indique clairement qui est hostile envers qui quand il note que «la chair ne se soumet pas à la loi de Dieu» (Rm 8:7) et que l'hostilité existe dans l'esprit en raison «des œuvres mauvaises» (Col 1,21).

Saint-Jean-Chrysostome note plus précisément: «Et qui demande-t-il? 'Réconciliez-vous avec Dieu.' Il ne dit pas: «réconciliez Dieu avec vous. Ce n'est pas lui qui nous hait, c'est vous qui voulez être ses ennemis. Dieu n'éprouve-t-il jamais un sentiment de haine[1]?» En effet, la voix active «réconcilier» (καταλλάξαι ou ἀποκαταλλάξαι), employée dans Colossiens 1,20 et ailleurs lorsque Paul parle de l'acte de Dieu comme la voix passive «être réconcilié» (καταλλάττεσθαι), employée lorsque Paul exhorte les chrétiens à se réconcilier avec Dieu, montre sans aucun doute que Dieu nous a réconciliés avec Lui.

Dieu réconcilie celles et ceux qui sont devenu-e-s les ennemi-e-s de Dieu, qui ont fait preuve d'ingratitude envers Lui. Et ces ennemi-e-s l'ont fait chaque fois qu'ils ont contribué aux conflits et aux guerres, aux inégalités sociales et économiques croissantes, à la crise climatique et à la pandémie de COVID-19. Le pardon de l'hostilité par la mort et la résurrection du Christ a offert la paix à tous les humains devenus ennemis à cause de leurs actes de péché.

Seul le Fils incarné, en qui il a plu «de faire habiter en lui toute la plénitude» (Col 1,19), peut rétablir la paix là où règne l'hostilité, peut rétablir la justice là où beaucoup souffrent encore de l'injustice, peut rétablir l'unité parmi celles et ceux qui sont obscurci-e-s par «idolâtrie, magie, haines, discorde, jalousie, emportements, rivalités, dissensions, factions».

L'être humain n'aurait jamais réussi par lui-même à atteindre la justice nécessaire à la réconciliation avec Dieu. Dans cette optique, l'apôtre Paul, au verset 20, relie le moment de la réconciliation à la mort du Christ sur la Croix («par le sang de sa croix»).

Le sang divin, versé sur la croix pour nous, par son pouvoir de pardonner l'hostilité, a fait la paix avec toutes choses, «et sur la terre et dans les cieux». De la même manière, la mort et la résurrection salvatrices du Christ apportent l'unité à toutes celles et à tous ceux qui sont touché-e-s par l'amour du Christ. Celles et ceux qui répudient l'amour égoïste, qui est la racine du péché, et apprennent de l'amour et de l'offrande désintéressée du Christ seront réconcilié-e-s par le Christ, même entre elles et eux. Ils ou elles répondront à la bonté et à la compassion du Christ en adoptant l'amour, la justice et la paix comme principes de comportement envers «toutes choses» et tous les humains, que le Christ aime et pour lesquels Il est mort.

Aujourd'hui, nous sommes appelé-e-s à exprimer notre gratitude pour l'amour du Christ pour notre monde et pour tous les êtres humains, et à réfléchir dans la prière et le repentir à notre réponse concrète à son amour. Nous voulons de tout cœur apprendre du sang de la croix que nous devons toutes et tous nous sacrifier et agir ensemble pour la justice, la paix et la réconciliation par le Christ, notre Seigneur de gloire béni.

---

1 Saint-Jean-Chrysostome, «Homilies on Second Corinthians» in New Advent, https://www.newadvent.org/fathers/2202.htm

- Comment l'amour du Christ nous mène-t-il à la justice et à l'unité? Qu'apprenons-nous de Son amour?
- Comment pouvons-nous faire preuve de gratitude en réponse à l'amour de Dieu? Quelles sont les actions concrètes d'amour envers les humains et l'ensemble de la création que Dieu nous pousse à entreprendre?

LE DESSEIN DE L'AMOUR DE DIEU DANS LE CHRIST POUR TOUTE LA CRÉATION: RÉCONCILIATION ET UNITÉ

Hyunju Bae

[35]Jésus parcourait toutes les villes et les villages, il y enseignait dans leurs synagogues, proclamant la Bonne Nouvelle du Royaume et guérissant toute maladie et toute infirmité. [36]Voyant les foules, il fut pris de pitié pour elles, parce qu'elles étaient harassées et prostrées comme des brebis qui n'ont pas de berger. [37]Alors il dit à ses disciples : «La moisson est abondante, mais les ouvriers peu nombreux ; [38]priez donc le maître de la moisson d'envoyer des ouvriers dans sa moisson».

—Matthieu 9,35-38

Jésus le compatissant

Matthieu 9,35-38 constitue un tournant. Ces versets reviennent sur le ministère de Jésus, tout en anticipant son enseignement sur la mission des disciples. Le verset 35 résume les actions de Jésus décrites en Matthieu 4,23 en répétant des termes comme enseigner, proclamer et guérir. Ces activités sont appelées le triple ministère de Jésus. Jésus a éclairé l'esprit des gens, les a invités à ouvrir leur cœur à l'avènement du Règne de Dieu et a guéri leurs maladies physiques.

Le verset 36 révèle que la compassion est la force motrice du ministère de Jésus. Jésus éprouvait de la compassion pour les gens qui étaient harassés et prostrés. «Harassé» (*eskylmenoi*) signifiait à l'origine être écorché ou dépecé. «Prostré» (*errimmenoi*) signifie être impuissant ou être allongé par terre. Les gens étaient exploités, déprimés, fatigués, abattus, écrasés. Jésus a répondu avec compassion aux gens, qui étaient comme des brebis qui n'ont pas de berger. Le verbe grec *splagchnizomai*, qui est employé dans Matthieu pour décrire la compassion de Jésus (14,14; 15,32; 18,27; 20,34), dérive du substantif *splagchnon*, dont le sens premier désigne les parties intérieures d'un corps ou les entrailles; le deuxième sens, le cœur; et le troisième, l'amour ou l'affection. La compassion que Jésus a manifestée dans ses actes de miséricorde (5,7; 9,13) découle spontanément de la capacité de l'amour à ressentir et à compatir dans les entrailles, c'est-à-dire de manière holistique en intégrant le cœur et le corps. La compassion est l'origine ultime du triple ministère de Jésus.

En 9,37, Jésus révèle son sens de la réalité en reconnaissant le déséquilibre entre une récolte abondante et le nombre restreint d'ouvriers. Cela ne conduit pas au désespoir, mais à la prise de conscience de l'occasion formidable et à la prière; dans le verset suivant, Jésus exhorte ses disciples à prier pour que le maître de la moisson envoie des ouvriers dans sa moisson. Cette section ouvre la voie à l'enseignement de Jésus sur l'obéissance au Christ et la mission au chapitre 10.

Jésus de Nazareth a vécu avec un cœur d'une compassion viscérale. Un contraste frappant avec le cœur compatissant est illustré de manière poignante dans la parabole de Jésus sur l'homme riche qui vit avec un cœur de pierre. Cet homme riche, «qui s'habillait de pourpre et de linge fin et qui faisait chaque jour de brillants festins», était apathique et aveugle aux besoins de Lazare, un pauvre homme qui gisait à sa porte, «couvert d'ulcères au porche de sa demeure. Il aurait bien voulu se rassasier de ce qui tombait de la table du riche; mais c'étaient plutôt les chiens qui venaient lécher ses ulcères». (Luc 16,9-21). À cause de son cœur inflexible, dur et égocentrique, l'homme riche ne pouvait pas voir Lazare, son proche voisin qui vivait dans une misère déshumanisante. Monopolisant l'abondance des biens, il ne fait pas progresser la vie des autres. Asservi par la cupidité, il ne comprend pas la sagesse de Jésus: Et il leur dit: «Attention! Gardez-vous de toute avidité; ce n'est pas du fait qu'un homme est riche qu'il a sa vie garantie par ses biens» (Luc 12,15). Certes, Lazare était considéré comme moins qu'humain en raison de sa condition physique, mais l'homme riche était dénué d'humanité dans une bien plus large mesure par son manque de conscience et son insensibilité à l'égard de son prochain. Le cœur de la compassion nous empêche de tomber dans le piège de la cupidité ou de nous dissimuler derrière le monde du dualisme, de l'abstraction et du calcul. La compassion est le cœur de l'amour du Christ et la lumière qui nous appelle à «imite[r] Dieu» (Ep 5,1). «Soyez généreux comme votre Père est généreux» (Luc 6,36).

Les signes de l'Anthropocène nous indiquent que l'humanité n'a pas d'avenir si nous ne faisons pas un effort concerté pour construire une civilisation de la compassion. Notre compassion doit être dirigée vers les personnes comme vers la nature. Un cœur humain cruel et insensible à son prochain ne se transformera pas du jour au lendemain en un cœur sensible à l'environnement. Comme l'a affirmé l'archevêque Desmond Tutu, «Une fois que nous aurons commencé à nous montrer respectueux-ses des personnes envers toute la famille de Dieu, nous serons également respectueux-ses de l'environnement.[2]». La foi chrétienne authentique peut faciliter ce processus, car elle est centrée sur Jésus, qui a apporté la paix sur la Terre et qui nous réconcilie à Dieu, les uns aux autres et à toute la création de Dieu (Ep 1,10; Col 1,15-20). Jésus a dit: «C'est un feu que je suis venu apporter sur la terre, et comme je voudrais qu'il soit déjà allumé!» (Luc 12,49). Le feu de la compassion, qui renforce le pouvoir relationnel des gens, constitue la base d'une nouvelle civilisation célébrant le tissu de la vie et la convivialité, car il peut façonner une contre-culture respectueuse de l'homme et de la nature.

La compassion est la qualité du leadership. La référence à «des brebis qui n'ont pas de berger» (Mt 9,36) évoque la mauvaise gestion des faux bergers qui se comportent en dirigeants infidèles. Elle fait écho à Ézéchiel 34, qui condamne les faux bergers d'Israël. Ils portent préjudice aux brebis en ne fortifiant pas la bête faible, en ne guérissant pas celle qui était malade, en ne faisant pas de bandage à celle qui était blessée, en ne ramenant pas celle qui s'écartait, en ne recherchant pas celle qui était perdue. Ils ont exercé leur autorité par la violence et l'oppression (Ez 34,4). Les faux bergers ne cherchent jamais les brebis dispersées pour éviter qu'elles ne deviennent de la nourriture pour tous les animaux sauvages (Ez 34,5-8). Jésus, le vrai berger de son peuple (Mt 2,6) est différent. Le premier verbe employé en Matthieu 9,35 indique que Jésus parcourait «en passant» toutes les villes et tous les villages (comme indiqué plus tôt, en Matthieu 4,23). Ce verbe, l'imparfait du grec *periagō*, désigne l'action répétée ou durative de Jésus. Jésus n'a pas mené une vie indifférente et égocentrique. Il est allé à la rencontre des gens sur le terrain pour voir leur situation de ses

2 Archevêque Desmond Tutu, «Foreword» dans *The Green Bible*, (San Francisco: Harper Bibles, 2010), I-13.

propres yeux. Car ainsi parle le Seigneur Dieu: «Je viens chercher moi-même mon troupeau pour en prendre soin» (Ez 34,11). Jésus, qui est un berger de David (Ez 34,23), est le vrai chef envoyé par Dieu.

Dans sa déclaration de novembre 2021 sur les résultats de la COP26, le Comité exécutif du COE a exhorté «toutes les Églises membres, les partenaires œcuméniques et les communautés chrétiennes à se comporter en leaders — et pas seulement en disciples — pour opérer les changements que nous appelons de nos vœux[3]». Lorsque l'exercice de la direction est requis de manière urgente à tous les niveaux de nos communautés dans la famille, l'Église et la société, la qualité de la direction compte. Elle devrait faciliter la vitesse de la *metanoia* à l'échelle de la civilisation et appeler la participation de toutes et tous. «Car la création attend avec impatience la révélation des fils de Dieu» (Rm 8,19). Le monde attend désormais les contributions actives et diverses de personnes éveillées de tous horizons, motivées par leur conscience et ayant le courage de changer. Dans le sillage de l'exhortation de Jésus, nous prions Dieu d'envoyer davantage d'ouvriers pour étendre le ministère urgent de guérison, de restauration, de réconciliation et d'unité afin de transformer notre monde meurtri. En tant que disciples de Jésus, nous sommes appelé-e-s à répondre à un appel urgent à revitaliser le ministère et la mission, rempli.es du feu de la compassion allumé par le mouvement de Jésus. Afin de répondre à cet appel, «nous voulons demeurer ensemble[4]». Nous continuerons de prier, de travailler et d'avancer ensemble, car nous souhaitons annoncer au monde la présence de Dieu, l'Emmanuel, au milieu de nous (Mt 1,23).

3 Comité exécutif du COE, Déclaration — Résultats de la COP26, 16 novembre 2021, https://www.oikoumene.org/fr/resources/documents/statement-on-the-outcome-of-cop26.

4 Message de la 1re Assemblée du Conseil œcuménique des Églises, Amsterdam, Pays-Bas, 1948. Lors de la 10e Assemblée, une invitation à un pèlerinage de justice et de paix a été formulée ainsi: «Nous voulons avancer ensemble» («Message de la Dixième Assemblée du COE»,Busan, République de Corée, du 30 octobre au 8 novembre 2013, https://www.oikoumene.org/fr/resources/documents/message-of-the-wcc-10th-assembly.

L'AMOUR DU CHRIST MÈNE LE MONDE À LA RÉCONCILIATION ET À L'UNITÉ

Krzysztof Mielcarek

25Et voici qu'un légiste se leva et lui dit, pour le mettre à l'épreuve: «Maître, que dois-je faire pour recevoir en partage la vie éternelle?» 26Jésus lui dit: «Dans la Loi qu'est-il écrit? Comment lis-tu? » 27Il lui répondit: «Tu aimeras le Seigneur ton Dieu de tout ton cœur, de toute ton âme, de toute ta force et de toute ta pensée, et ton prochain comme toi-même». 28Jésus lui dit: « Tu as bien répondu. Fais cela et tu auras la vie».29Mais lui, voulant montrer sa justice, dit à Jésus: «Et qui est mon prochain?» 30Jésus reprit: «Un homme descendait de Jérusalem à Jéricho, il tomba sur des bandits qui, l'ayant dépouillé et roué de coups, s'en allèrent, le laissant à moitié mort. 31Il se trouva qu'un prêtre descendait par ce chemin; il vit l'homme et passa à bonne distance. 32Un lévite de même arriva en ce lieu; il vit l'homme et passa à bonne distance. 33Mais un Samaritain qui était en voyage arriva près de l'homme: il le vit et fut pris de pitié. 34Il s'approcha, banda ses plaies en y versant de l'huile et du vin, le chargea sur sa propre monture, le conduisit à une auberge et prit soin de lui. 35Le lendemain, tirant deux pièces d'argent, il les donna à l'aubergiste et lui dit: "Prends soin de lui, et si tu dépenses quelque chose de plus, c'est moi qui te le rembourserai quand je repasserai". 36Lequel des trois, à ton avis, s'est montré le prochain de l'homme qui était tombé sur les bandits?» 37Le légiste répondit: «C'est celui qui a fait preuve de bonté envers lui». Jésus lui dit: «Va et, toi aussi, fais de même».
—Luc 10,25-37

«Maître, que dois-je faire pour recevoir en partage la vie éternelle?» «Dans la Loi, qu'est-il écrit? Comment lis-tu?» Le dialogue préliminaire de Jésus avec le scribe nous amène au cœur de la péricope que nous venons de lire. Puisque la vie éternelle dépend de notre amour de Dieu et de nos prochains, pour un chrétien, il n'y a pas de sujet plus important que cet engagement. Chaque israélite pieux rappelait cette vérité fondamentale en récitant chaque jour le *Chema Israël*. Le scribe, cependant, porte le dialogue à un niveau supérieur, car il demande à Jésus d'identifier les objets de son amour. Il n'y a aucune difficulté avec le premier parce qu'il s'agit de Dieu. Mais qui est le prochain? Cette question est au cœur de la parabole citée par Jésus et est intimement liée à son protagoniste.

Bien que la tradition biblique ait appelé cette histoire «la parabole du bon Samaritain », la figure qui unit tous ses héros n'est pas un Samaritain, mais un pauvre homme qui, en descendant de Jérusalem à Jéricho, est attaqué par des brigands. La parabole commence avec lui, et il est présent jusqu'à la fin. Bien que le narrateur ne nous raconte pas cette histoire de son point de vue, il est néanmoins au cœur de la parabole. C'est lui qui peut être identifié avec le prochain sur lequel le scribe s'interroge. Pour paraphraser d'autres paraboles du maître de Nazareth, on pourrait dire que chaque prochain dans le besoin est comme un homme attaqué par des brigands.

En donnant cette interprétation d'un prochain, Jésus élargit consciemment le concept biblique du terme hébreu *rē'a* ou grec *plesíon*, qui signifiait généralement un ami ou un voisin. Le récit ne mentionne cependant pas que le prêtre, le lévite ou le Samaritain connaissaient la victime à l'avance. Ainsi, le personnage principal de la parabole répond à tous les critères de l'inconnu[5]. En fait, la construction de la parabole renforce progressivement la distance entre l'attaqué et les trois passants. En effet, le verset 30 donne à penser qu'il s'agit d'un pèlerin juif qui rentre chez lui après avoir visité le Sanctuaire de Jérusalem. Cela suggère au moins une sorte de lien formel entre lui et le personnel du temple. Au contraire, les deux le voient sur la route, et non seulement ils passent leur chemin, mais ils traversent même (*antiparerchomai*) pour ne pas s'approcher de la victime de l'agression. Ainsi, ils s'éloignent de la personne dans le besoin[6].

Par ailleurs, le Samaritain est l'incarnation de l'étrangeté pour l'homme attaqué[7]. Ce dernier, probablement un juif fervent, aurait considéré tous les Samaritains comme des renégats[8]. La haine était réciproque; ainsi, nous pouvons mettre en évidence une distance extrême entre les personnages. Or, le Samaritain franchit la barrière de l'hostilité et du ressentiment.

La parabole de Jésus attire l'attention de l'auditeur sur les actions du Samaritain: il voit un homme dans le besoin et est ému par sa situation. La compassion du Samaritain, cependant, n'est pas une simple émotion vide, car il entreprend d'autres actions concrètes. Il s'approche de la victime, panse ses blessures, la conduit à une auberge, la soigne et paie les frais nécessaires à son rétablissement. Vous remarquerez que Jésus ne partage pas avec son auditoire la possible fin heureuse de l'histoire, laissant planer un certain doute. Ainsi, son attention est entièrement focalisée sur l'attitude du Samaritain envers la victime, à savoir qu'il a fait tout ce qu'il pouvait pour prendre soin de cet homme.

L'expression «tout ce qu'il pouvait» nécessite un bref commentaire. La juxtaposition du Samaritain avec Jésus conduit de nombreux prédicateurs à exagérer son attitude miséricordieuse pour en faire un dévouement total. Il convient toutefois de noter que l'épilogue de la parabole apporte un autre éclairage. Le Samaritain reprend finalement ses activités quotidiennes, laissant le blessé aux soins du propriétaire de l'auberge (versets 10,35). Il ne subordonne pas toute sa vie à la victime du vol, mais apporte son soutien à l'homme, à la mesure de ses besoins.

Quelles sont les conséquences du message de Jésus pour les chrétiens d'aujourd'hui? Elles peuvent être exprimées en plusieurs points:

1. Vous pouvez être confronté-e à une situation dans laquelle votre prochain a un besoin soudain.

5 Hébreu: ***ben-nēḵar/'iš-noḵri/gēr/*** *zār*, Grec: *allótrios/allogenēs/pároikos*. Voir Genèse 17,12-27; 42,7; Esther 8,12; 1 Michée 12,10; Job 28,4; Psaume 35,15; 105,12; 109,11; Proverbes 5,10; 8,8; 14,10; 27,2; Ecclésiaste 6,2; Siracide 32,18; Ésaïe 61,5; Jérémie 14,8; 51,51; Osée 7,9; 8,7; Joel 4,17; Abdias 1,11; Éphésiens 2,12; 4,18.

6 Dans l'attitude du prêtre et du lévite, certains voient le désir d'éviter la contamination rituelle, tandis que d'autres y voient le dégoût pour un homme battu.

7 Les commentateurs font remarquer que le contenu de cette parabole a dû choquer l'auditoire de Jésus. On trouve d'autres exemples de ce type dans l'Évangile selon Luc: voir, par exemple, la purification des lépreux par Jésus (Luc 17,11-19).

8 Les origines du peuple samaritain sont associées à la conquête d'Israël par l'Assyrie (722 avant notre ère). Une partie de la population du royaume est alors déplacée en Mésopotamie, et à sa place, s'installe une population étrangère de culture et de croyances différentes (2 R 17,24-41). Au fil du temps, elle a été assimilée et ses croyances ont fusionné avec celles des israélites. Cela a donné naissance à une religion éclectique dont le centre se trouve au sommet du mont Garizim. Les différences entre Juifs et Samaritains ont provoqué un ressentiment mutuel (voir Jean 4,9; *Talmud Jerušalaim: Shekalim* 1.4.3; *Shevi'it* 6.1.16; 8.8.1).

2. L’appartenance à des institutions religieuses ne garantit pas une attitude appropriée envers les personnes dans le besoin.
3. Sans tenir compte des jugements négatifs des autres, agissez selon ce qui est bon et juste.
4. Aidez toute personne dans le besoin, même si cela vous prive temporairement d’un certain confort personnel, de biens ou de temps.
5. Agissez de manière adéquate pour satisfaire les besoins de votre prochain.

Le monde moderne ne nous permet pas d’envisager cette parabole uniquement du point de vue d’une personne individuelle. Aujourd’hui, des nations entières, voire des continents, souffrent, ce qui appelle une réponse systémique et mondiale. De nombreuses organisations religieuses et internationales ont été créées pour venir en aide aux victimes d’aujourd’hui. D’énormes disparités de richesse et de niveau de vie ont provoqué des vagues de migration de personnes en quête de meilleures conditions de vie. Une série de conflits régionaux sanglants a chassé un grand nombre de réfugié-e-s de leur foyer. Les pays et les régions prospères doivent donc prendre des mesures concrètes pour soulager la misère des victimes de ces phénomènes désastreux. Les dernières décennies nous ont montré des exemples à la fois d’une générosité héroïque sans précédent et d’une froide indifférence. Nous devons par conséquent prier pour que la communauté internationale apprenne de ses erreurs et adopte des mesures efficaces. Les Églises individuelles, notamment celles qui jouissent d’une portée mondiale, ont également un rôle important à jouer.

Néanmoins, le point de départ pour chacun-e devrait être de se poser la question: dans quelle mesure suis-je le prochain d’une autre personne? Dans quelle mesure est-ce que je me comporte en prochain? La parabole de Jésus est une sorte de cri, un appel à se comporter en prochain, même si cela signifie renoncer à une partie de notre propre confort, de nos biens et de notre temps.

La réponse de Jésus à la question du scribe est, *de facto*, «TOUT LE MONDE». Le ou la disciple du Christ est donc appelé-e à faire tomber les barrières religieuses, culturelles et politiques et à tendre la main à celles et ceux qui sont dans le besoin. Le thème de cette Assemblée, «L’amour du Christ mène le monde à la réconciliation et à l’unité», peut être paraphrasé ainsi: «la miséricorde du Christ nous amène à découvrir notre prochain dans chaque être humain.»

L'AMOUR DU CHRIST — COMPASSION POUR LA VIE — AFFIRMER LA PLÉNITUDE DE LA VIE

Diana Tsaghikyan

[1]En passant, Jésus vit un homme aveugle de naissance. [2]Ses disciples lui posèrent cette question: «Rabbi, qui a péché pour qu'il soit né aveugle, lui ou ses parents?» [3]Jésus répondit: «Ni lui, ni ses parents. Mais c'est pour que les œuvres de Dieu se manifestent en lui! [4]Tant qu'il fait jour, il nous faut travailler aux œuvres de celui qui m'a envoyé: la nuit vient où personne ne peut travailler; [5]aussi longtemps que je suis dans le monde, je suis la lumière du monde».[6]Ayant ainsi parlé, Jésus cracha à terre, fit de la boue avec la salive et l'appliqua sur les yeux de l'aveugle; [7]et il lui dit: «Va te laver à la piscine de Siloé» – ce qui signifie Envoyé. L'aveugle y alla, il se lava et, à son retour, il voyait.[8]Les gens du voisinage et ceux qui auparavant avaient l'habitude de le voir – car c'était un mendiant – disaient: «N'est-ce pas celui qui était assis à mendier?» [9]Les uns disaient: «C'est bien lui!» D'autres disaient: «Mais non, c'est quelqu'un qui lui ressemble». Mais l'aveugle affirmait: «C'est bien moi».[10]Ils lui dirent donc: «Et alors, tes yeux, comment se sont-ils ouverts?» [11]Il répondit: «L'homme qu'on appelle Jésus a fait de la boue, m'en a frotté les yeux et m'a dit: "Va à Siloé et lave-toi". Alors moi, j'y suis allé, je me suis lavé et j'ai retrouvé la vue». [12]Ils lui dirent: «Où est-il, celui-là?» Il répondit: «Je n'en sais rien».
—Jean 9,1-12

On considère généralement la guérison de l'aveugle comme un miracle. Jésus a vu un aveugle et, étonnamment, a permis à cet homme de voir. En fait, la guérison de l'aveugle était un miracle. Des miracles se sont produits à l'époque, et des miracles se produisent de diverses manières aujourd'hui aussi. Or, cette histoire n'est pas seulement celle d'un miracle, mais aussi celle de l'amour du Christ et du pouvoir de la compassion.

Que savons-nous du mendiant? Cet homme avait des parents, mais était seul; il vivait dans la société, mais en était exclu. Aveugle de naissance, il n'a jamais vu la lumière jusqu'à ce que le Christ le voie et change sa réalité. Tout d'abord, nous lisons que Jésus voit un aveugle, et nous sommes immédiatement témoins de la façon dont Jésus rejette le dicton «Aveugle et boiteux n'entreront pas dans la Maison» (2 Sm 5,8). Jésus corrige les idées fausses de ses disciples sur le péché et la souffrance, les instruit sur l'œuvre de Dieu et les éclaire en déclarant: «[A]ussi longtemps que je suis dans le monde, je suis la lumière du monde.» Puis Jésus fait de la boue avec sa salive, l'applique sur les yeux de l'aveugle et lui dit: «Va te laver à la piscine de Siloé.» Après avoir suivi ces instructions, le mendiant revient, capable de voir.

Un miracle incroyable vient de se produire, mais personne ne semble heureux ni intéressé par l'ancien aveugle. Nous sommes peut-être témoins de l'indifférence au lieu des soins et de la compassion attendus. Fait intéressant, dans les questions posées par les autres, nous ne voyons personne essayer de découvrir ses émotions et ses sentiments nouvellement éprouvés. Il est accueilli par l'indifférence plutôt que par l'attention et la compassion. En revanche, Jésus, avec son amour et sa grâce absolus, guérit un aveugle qui était exclu et marginalisé. Jésus remet en question la société et agit. Il offre au mendiant un profond sentiment d'espoir et une conscience plus profonde du pouvoir salvateur de Dieu. Il restaure la plénitude de la vie de l'homme en lui assignant un nouveau but et une nouvelle direction. Jésus donne à l'homme la vision de la lumière.

La déception, la frustration et l'absence de vision de la vie peuvent assombrir par l'incertitude notre vie actuelle et nos espoirs futurs, mais en une période d'obscurité, il est impératif d'avoir une vision de lumière. Nous ne pouvons pas rester dans la grotte de la mort, où l'intelligence est réduite au silence, et dans laquelle on ne trouve ni piété ni compassion. Aujourd'hui plus que jamais — après 2022 années — les Églises chrétiennes sont toujours confrontées à de nombreux défis. Des remèdes précieux pour guérir les blessures du corps du Christ sont nécessaires. La compassion doit être la réponse.

La véritable compassion trouve une belle signification dans la façon dont nous traitons les autres. Elle a le pouvoir de faire avancer l'humanité vers un chemin juste où l'amour du Christ est explicité et où la lumière est vue. Une compassion authentique change notre mode de vie. Lorsque nous adoptons la compassion dans nos vies, nous essayons de faire preuve de miséricorde et de patience, d'être plein-e-s d'espoir et fidèles. Dans les moments d'impatience, nous devons nous rappeler que Dieu œuvre de manière mystérieuse. Nous devons apprécier la façon dont la compassion nous rappelle ce que signifie notre humanité.

Cette histoire, par chacun de ses aspects, a des implications spirituelles; elle fournit un parallèle puissant au rôle de Dieu qui nous amène à la foi et au salut par la grâce et le pouvoir de la compassion. La compassion est une qualité fondamentale du concept biblique de Dieu. Jésus-Christ, en qui Dieu a été «manifesté dans la chair» (1 Tm 3,16), constitue un exemple remarquable de compassion. Jésus a enseigné que la compassion doit s'étendre, non seulement aux ami-e-s et aux prochains, mais à tout le monde sans exception, à l'ensemble de la race humaine. L'évangéliste Jean veut que nous restaurions et conservions notre vision de la lumière.

Toutes les époques connaissent des impératifs. À notre époque matérialiste et laïque, dans le contexte d'une pandémie sanitaire mondiale, alors que nous sommes confronté-e-s à l'horrible réalité du racisme, de la discrimination, de la pauvreté, de la violence, de l'instabilité politique, des guerres et du changement climatique, il est absolument indispensable de ne pas baisser les bras. Nous devons plus que jamais valoriser les aspects spirituels de nos vies. Chacun-e d'entre nous est unique (nous avons des opinions, des cultures, des expériences et des origines différentes), mais notre foi mutuelle dans le Christ et notre amour pour le Seigneur nous unissent. Par-dessus tout, il y a l'unité de service et de témoignage dans le monde entier au nom de Jésus-Christ, qui est «la lumière du monde». La vie semble dénuée d'espoir sans une relation vivante avec notre Créateur et avec les autres. Jésus-Christ a ouvert le chemin de d'amour de la vie bénie, et ce chemin lumineux et porteur de vie nous rendra fort-e-s, confiant-e-s que chacun-e de nous a une raison de vivre et de créer. Notre Seigneur Jésus-Christ a donné à l'humanité l'espoir et la grâce d'affronter la souffrance et d'hériter de la vie éternelle.

Je crois qu'avec un respect mutuel et la ferme conviction que le Christ est ressuscité, nous répandrons la parole de Dieu. Nous continuerons humblement de rechercher la lumière de Dieu et d'œuvrer à la réconciliation et à l'unité. Nous chérirons notre dessein individuel et, après l'avoir trouvé, nous ferons preuve d'un immense respect à l'égard de la diversité de notre humanité. Ce dessein s'accompagne de la responsabilité d'agir avec compassion, avec l'amour du Christ dans nos esprits et nos âmes, et avec sa lumière indéfectible comme guide. Cependant, nous ne pouvons accomplir aucun de ces actes par nous-mêmes: nous avons besoin les uns des autres. Ensemble, nous pouvons nous souvenir de notre passé, vivre notre présent et créer notre avenir. Nous voulons être ensemble; n'est-ce pas un miracle?

> «Lumière, et source d'illumination,
> abritée par une lumière inaccessible…
> Dans l'aube de la lumière du matin,
> apporte aussi la lumière de la compréhension dans nos âmes[9]».

9 Nerses Shnorhali (Saint Nerses le Gracieux) était l'un des plus remarquables théologiens médiévaux et la figure œcuménique par excellence de l'histoire de l'Église arménienne. La citation ci-dessus est extraite de son «Hymne à la lumière» (*Luys ararich Luso*).

L'AMOUR DU CHRIST — TRANSFORMER L'OBÉISSANCE AU CHRIST — AFFIRMER LA JUSTICE ET LA DIGNITÉ HUMAINE

Paulo Ueti

21Partant de là, Jésus se retira dans la région de Tyr et de Sidon. 22Et voici qu'une Cananéenne vint de là et elle se mit à crier: «Aie pitié de moi, Seigneur, Fils de David ! Ma fille est cruellement tourmentée par un démon». 23Mais il ne lui répondit pas un mot. Ses disciples, s'approchant, lui firent cette demande: «Renvoie-la, car elle nous poursuit de ses cris».24Jésus répondit: «Je n'ai été envoyé qu'aux brebis perdues de la maison d'Israël». 25Mais la femme vint se prosterner devant lui: «Seigneur, dit-elle, viens à mon secours!» 26Il répondit: «Il n'est pas bien de prendre le pain des enfants pour le jeter aux petits chiens». 27«C'est vrai, Seigneur! reprit-elle; et justement les petits chiens mangent des miettes qui tombent de la table de leurs maîtres».28Alors Jésus lui répondit: «Femme, ta foi est grande! Qu'il t'arrive comme tu le veux!» Et sa fille fut guérie dès cette heure-là.

—Matthieu 15,21-28

La version de Matthieu de cette histoire, qui comporte plus d'éléments que la version de Marc 7, 24-30 est encore plus provocatrice, car elle intègre les disciples de Jésus au récit. Nous savons que l'Évangile de Matthieu a été écrit vers 80-90 de notre ère, reflétant non seulement les événements de l'époque de Jésus en Palestine, mais aussi ce qui se passait dans l'Église de Syrie, origine probable de la plupart des écrits de cette communauté.

Ce texte traite de la communauté: qui nous accueillons et comment nous les accueillons. Et comme il s'agit d'un texte sur la communauté, c'est une provocation sur les habitudes d'accueil, de réconciliation, et de vie en harmonie dans le Christ Jésus. Des personnes de cultures, de langues, de milieux, d'habitudes, de genres, d'âges et de positions de pouvoir différents se retrouvent dans un contexte de violence sexiste, de racisme, de besoin, de douleur, de maladie, d'exclusion, de xénophobie et de préjugés.

Cependant, il est toujours impératif de nous souvenir que Dieu «aime l'émigré» (Deut 10,18). Lorsque nous lisons l'ensemble des textes du canon biblique, nous constatons que l'esprit de la Torah et des prophètes est très présent également dans le Nouveau Testament: celui-ci prône la protection des personnes confrontées à l'oppression, à la maladie, à l'exclusion et à la violence, et de celles qui sont défavorisées dans le système et éprouvent un besoin qui les fait percevoir comme moins humaines. Les pauvres, les étrangers, les orphelins, les veuves, les enfants et les femmes font partie des personnes qui ont le plus besoin d'être protégées.

Le texte déploie la méthodologie dialogique d'une femme étrangère dans sa rencontre avec Jésus, le juif. Elle est cananéenne et de culture hélléniste. Le fait qu'elle soit une «étrangère» paraît pertinent pour l'auteur de cette histoire. Il semble y avoir un problème dans la communauté par rapport au dialogue, aux relations et à l'accueil des inconnue-e-s, des étrangers et des étrangères, ainsi que des femmes à la table de communion. Nous savons qu'une table partagée, *koinonia*, est une procuration pour le culte, pour célébrer et reconnaître Jésus qui chemine avec nous. La table partagée guérit et nous rassemble, ou devrait le faire.

Nous remarquons l'intérêt des auteur-e-s à mettre en avant les deux femmes, la fille et la mère, toutes deux sans nom. La scène est présentée comme une rencontre, pas très amicale au début, entre deux personnes qui normalement n'échangeraient pas de regard, et n'engageraient encore moins une conversation. Pour de nombreuses personnes de l'époque, les non-juifs étaient considérés comme des «chiens», tout comme les non-Romains étaient des barbares. Néanmoins, la rencontre a lieu. Un débat s'engage, apparemment entre personnes inégales, mais lorsque nous analysons le discours, nous percevons que les deux sont au même niveau en termes de volonté d'engagement, de technique et de contenu. La femme n'est pas totalement soumise. Elle s'investit, est intelligente, résiliente et persévérante pour parvenir à ses fins.

La conversation s'engage à cause de la maladie de la fille de cette femme, de ses attentes à l'égard de Jésus, et de son audace à interrompre le désir de Jésus de rester anonyme. La femme affronte cet homme qui ne veut pas prêter attention à son besoin, et elle fait face à l'impolitesse et au manque d'empathie des disciples. Selon Matthieu, elle «se mit à crier». Imaginez la scène embarrassante d'une femme criant sur quelqu'un qui veut garder l'anonymat. Lorsqu'il est confronté, Jésus exprime sa position, issue de sa tradition culturelle, de ce qu'il a appris dans son enfance et de son éducation. Il refuse de partager le pain et la table — une métaphore de la communauté, un groupe de soutien. Il semble que la communauté de Matthieu ait un problème concernant le droit d'accès à la table.

Pour en revenir à l'intrigue, il est intéressant de noter les questions qui imprègnent le dialogue de ces deux personnes de cultures différentes: une rencontre entre personnes inégales; esprit impur/besoin; pain en haut/miettes en bas; au-dessus de la table/en dessous de la table. Ils semblent parler de sujets différents, sans rapport. La femme, Grecque par son éducation, a ses besoins (guérir sa fille, chasser le démon, récupérer sa fille, obtenir de l'aide, s'inscrire dans l'univers linguistique de Jésus). Jésus, quant à lui, est intransigeant sur le plan culturel (ethnocentrique et intolérant), et il tente de l'empêcher d'accéder à la table. Dans le récit de Matthieu, là encore les disciples demandent à Jésus: «Renvoie-la» — ce qui peut signifier «prendre en charge» ou «la renvoyer sans la prendre en charge» — mais dans tous les cas, les intermédiaires sont gênés par cette relation. Dans la communauté de Matthieu, il semble que la femme ne devrait pas avoir le droit d'accéder à la table, c'est-à-dire à Jésus.

La question fondamentale de la femme, développée avec convenance et habileté rhétorique, est la suivante: qui a accès à Jésus? Qui peut atteindre le pain? Est-ce seulement les enfants d'Israël, ceux du monde de Jésus et les disciples; ceux qui sont préparés; ceux qui sont exempts du péché? Les deux textes indiquent que c'étaient la pensée et la parole initiales de Jésus. Or, la femme n'a pas accepté cette norme culturelle et sociale. Elle n'aimait pas vivre dans un monde où la norme consistait à exclure les gens comme elle et son espèce. Elle a transgressé le langage homogène et dominant de cette culture, de cette tradition et de cette religion, et a fait en sorte que cet homme change d'avis et d'attitude. Elle a produit des connaissances, jetant les bases d'une nouvelle possibilité épistémologique: «Par la bouche des tout-petits et des nourrissons, tu as fondé une forteresse» (Ps 8,3).

Il est également intéressant, au vu du contexte littéraire, que ce texte se trouve entre deux autres textes qui mentionnent le pain:

Matthieu 14,13-21. Premier partage des pains aux 5 000; il reste 12 paniers.
Matthieu 15,21-28. Notre histoire contradictoire sur qui peut avoir accès à Jésus/au pain/aux miettes.
Matthieu 15, 15,32-38. Second partage des pains aux 4 000; il reste 7 paniers.

Nous trouvons la corrélation dans Marc ainsi que dans Matthieu. Il semble que de l'histoire de la femme syrophénicienne, qui s'est disputée avec Jésus pour savoir qui pouvait avoir accès au pain ou obtenir la guérison, ait découlé la nécessité de raconter à nouveau le premier récit de la multiplication des pains et de lui donner une autre fin, en affirmant que tout le monde a accès à Jésus. Il est bon de rappeler ici qu'avoir accès à Jésus, c'est avoir accès à la communauté, à un nouveau projet, à un espace politique et idéo-théologique qui va à contre-courant de ce qui était établi jusqu'à présent et encore aujourd'hui.

Tout le monde a accès à Jésus/à la table/à la communion/à la communauté/au dialogue

> Il n'y a plus ni Juif, ni Grec; il n'y a plus ni esclave, ni homme libre;
> Il n'y a plus l'homme et la femme;
> car tous, vous n'êtes qu'un en Jésus Christ.
>
> **—Galates 3,28**

L'accès à Jésus, au pain ou aux miettes qui tombent de la table, est lié aux rencontres et aux décalages entre des personnes de cultures différentes, qui ont des lexiques différents, et des besoins et désirs variés d'apprendre les uns des autres. Voilà pourquoi notre épisode insiste tant sur la culture et la géographie des deux personnages et sur leurs besoins: la femme et la fille en manque de relations et de participation (pain, table, santé, communion, soutien, reconnaissance), et Jésus et ses plus proches disciples (des hommes, il faut le préciser), piégés par un ethnocentrisme culturel à l'origine de xénophobie et de violence. Néanmoins, ces hommes ont reçu la capacité d'écouter et, même en cas de désaccord, de surmonter leur prétendue supériorité et de rester ouvert au dialogue jusqu'à la fin. Il semble que ce n'est que dans un processus dialogique que la santé et la vie peuvent apparaître. Il faut peut-être y voir un avertissement à la communauté: l'ouverture à de nouvelles relations, l'écoute spirituelle et vocationnelle, la solidarité, le sens de l'équité et le partage sont nécessaires pour transformer les désaccords en rencontres d'amour et de vie. De telles rencontres évitent la maladie et la mort et nous transforment. Dans 1 Corinthiens 11,28-32, Paul a condamné la pratique du souper dans la communauté corinthienne, le fait de manger sans jugement préalable de soi-même. Aujourd'hui, on compte un grand nombre de personnes malades et faibles; certaines sont déjà mortes parce que la communauté ne les a pas soutenues - d'où l'exhortation à faire son propre examen pour ne pas s'autocondamner.

Il nous faut «désapprendre». «Mais ce qui est folie dans le monde, Dieu l'a choisi pour confondre les sages; ce qui est faible dans le monde, Dieu l'a choisi pour confondre ce qui est fort» (1 Cor. 1,27-28). Jésus, ou la communauté, a désappris quelque chose afin d'appréhender beaucoup plus. Les rencontres entre différentes cultures provoquent ce résultat lorsque nous sommes vraiment ouvert-e-s et disposé-e-s à aller dans le sens d'un détachement de nos vérités, traditions et certitudes. De cette façon, nous pouvons prêter attention à l'attitude fondamentale de notre spiritualité de libération: écouter le Dieu qui donne la vie et vient à nous dans un monde pluriel et diversifié et Lui obéir.

La femme n'est pas découragée par le problème de ne pas être prise en charge. Elle est une victime, mais n'est pas passive. Elle a des droits, et la conscience qu'elle en a lui donne la force (dynamo) d'aller de l'avant (affronter). Même depuis sa condition de «chien» (qu'elle revendique en effet), elle affirme que ce n'est pas un problème qui peut l'empêcher de participer pleinement à la communion.

Ce récit, à mon avis, rejoint d'autres qui soulignent la nécessité pour notre mentalité, nos théologies, nos pratiques et notre pastorale d'être antiracistes, antixénophobes et contre toute forme de violence. De même, il nous appelle à prendre en charge, sans condition, celles et ceux qui ont besoin d'aide et à prêter attention aux conflits que cela peut provoquer dans la communauté ecclésiale et aussi dans notre maison commune, l'*oikoumène* et au niveau de la planète. Cherchons-nous le dialogue et restons-nous dans le dialogue, même lorsque nous sommes offensé-e-s, disqualifié-e-s et diminué-e-s dans notre humanité? Comment pouvons-nous en faire une pratique qui s'étend aux environnements et aux contextes dans lesquels nous vivons?

Aller à la rencontre des autres représente toujours un défi. Mais il s'agit de notre appel. Sommes-nous à l'écoute, comme le semeur de la parabole[10] de l'appel à semer, quelle que soit la difficulté du sol?

Puisse la Trinité nous bénir avec l'esprit d'indignation et de résilience caractéristique de notre spiritualité.

---

10 Matthieu 13,3-8; Marc 4,3-8; Luc 8,5-8.

L'AMOUR DU CHRIST: LE LIEN DE L'UNITÉ CHRÉTIENNE ET LE TÉMOIGNAGE COMMUN DES ÉGLISES

Kenneth Mtata

[20]Alors la mère des fils de Zébédée s'approcha de lui, avec ses fils, et elle se prosterna pour lui faire une demande. [21]Il lui dit: «Que veux-tu?» – «Ordonne, lui dit-elle, que dans ton Royaume mes deux fils que voici siègent l'un à ta droite et l'autre à ta gauche». [22]Jésus répondit: «Vous ne savez pas ce que vous demandez. Pouvez-vous boire la coupe que je vais boire?» Ils lui disent: «Nous le pouvons». [23]Il leur dit: «Ma coupe, vous la boirez; quant à siéger à ma droite et à ma gauche, il ne m'appartient pas de l'accorder: ce sera donné à ceux pour qui mon Père l'a préparé». [24]Les dix, qui avaient entendu, s'indignèrent contre les deux frères. [25]Mais Jésus les appela et leur dit: «Vous le savez, les chefs des nations les tiennent sous leur pouvoir et les grands sous leur domination. [26]Il ne doit pas en être ainsi parmi vous. Au contraire, si quelqu'un veut être grand parmi vous, qu'il soit votre serviteur, [27]et si quelqu'un veut être le premier parmi vous, qu'il soit votre esclave. [28]C'est ainsi que le Fils de l'homme est venu non pour être servi, mais pour servir et donner sa vie en rançon pour la multitude».

—Matthieu 20,20-28

La mère des deux fils de Zébédée s'approche de Jésus dans la posture la plus révérencieuse, proche de l'adoration (προσκυνοῦσα), pour implorer une faveur pour ses deux fils. Bien que les fils soient connus sous le nom de leur père, Zébédée, elle utilise son autorité matriarcale afin de plaider en faveur de leur exaltation. Voilà qui est typique de ces cultures traditionnelles où le leadership explicite est patriarcal, mais où le pouvoir réel est déterminé de manière matriarcale, hors de la vue du public. En tout cas, elle poursuit pour ses fils ce que l'Évangile de Matthieu présente comme son objectif ultime: «Cherchez d'abord le Royaume et la justice de Dieu, et tout cela vous sera donné par surcroît» (6,33).

Qu'est-ce qui éclaire sa compréhension du «royaume»? Certains chercheurs ont préféré lire la référence de Matthieu au royaume dans le contexte de la «communauté chrétienne juive en train de redéfinir sa propre identité face à l'opposition juive, qui se consolidait sous la direction des pharisiens-scribes[11].» D'autres considèrent l'ensemble de l'Évangile selon Matthieu en général et le langage de royaume en particulier dans le contexte plus large de la domination et du pouvoir impériaux romains[12]. Les deux insistances ne sont pas forcément mutuellement exclusives. C'est bien connu que les Romains, avec leur présence concentrée à Antioche, ont influé sur le contexte social des

11 A. B. Du Toit, «The Kingdom of God in the Gospel of Matthew», *Skrif en Kerk* 21, no. 3 (2000), 545.

12 Boris Repschinsk, «Kingdoms of the Earth and the Kingdom of the Heavens: Matthew's Perspective on Political Power», dans *The Composition, Theology, and Early Reception of Matthew's Gospel*, éd. Joseph Verheyden, Jens Schröter et David C. Sim (Tübingen: Mohr Siebeck, 2022), 149.

communautés derrière l'Évangile de Matthieu. Ces Romains sont les «Gentils» qui viennent immédiatement à l'esprit. Ils ont exercé un pouvoir dominateur sur leurs sujets colonisés par le biais d'une administration politique de substitution complaisante, mais aussi par leur présence militaire et leur domination religieuse. À cet égard, les Romains exerçaient réellement le «pouvoir sur» (κατακυριεύουσιν) leurs sujets. Et comme tous les peuples colonisés, les disciples et leurs communautés étaient attirés par les excès de pouvoir démontrés par l'oppresseur romain et l'imitaient. Il n'est donc pas surprenant qu'ils cherchent à créer leurs propres petits empires, caractérisés par un «pouvoir dominateur » et des relations tyranniques. Vu sous cet angle, la mère des fils de Zébédée cherche à obtenir des positions de choix pour ses fils. Ce faisant, elle espère également se réserver une place spéciale dans le royaume.

Cependant, Jésus propose une redéfinition du pouvoir en tant que pouvoir exercé dans le sacrifice et l'humilité (Matthieu 20,26-27). C'est dans une conception de ce type que le royaume de Dieu est le mieux compris — où la grandeur est démontrée en étant un serviteur (διάκονος) et même un esclave (δοῦλος), où ce service pourrait aller jusqu'à la mort. Dans le contexte littéraire immédiat du passage d'aujourd'hui, Jésus prédit sa mort (17-19) et guérit les deux aveugles (par opposition aux deux fils de Zébédée?) en passant par Jéricho (29-34). La mort de Jésus est ce qui ouvre les yeux sur la vraie grandeur. Jésus n'est pas seulement le maître, mais aussi l'exemple ultime de diaconie, ou de service dans l'humilité.

Que cela signifie-t-il pour nous?

«Les dix, qui avaient entendu, s'indignèrent contre les deux frères» (v. 24). Mary Jane Gorman explique: «Nous pouvons nous identifier à la colère des dix autres disciples: si nous avons vertueusement résisté à demander à nous asseoir à côté de l'invité d'honneur, nous pourrions en vouloir à quelqu'un d'autre qui l'a demandé[13].» De même que l'unité des disciples était menacée par cet acte de pouvoir égocentrique, de même, l'unité de l'Église souffre sous le poids d'un pouvoir dominateur, autoritaire et privilégié, car il engendre à son tour des réactions de colère, de jalousie et de méfiance.

Tout comme dans le contexte de l'Empire romain, des formes de pouvoir militariste, exclusiviste et idolâtre semblent peser sur le monde d'aujourd'hui. Cette expression du pouvoir oppressif peut se perpétuer par des alliances patriarcales et matriarcales trompeuses (une mère préparant une place spéciale pour ses fils), des idéologies absolutistes de gauche et de droite (l'un à droite et l'autre à gauche), ou des identités raciales ou ethniques relevant du népotisme (fils de Zébédée), le tout sous couvert de religiosité et de piété (recherche du Royaume de Dieu).

L'unité de l'Église, explique Jésus, peut être maintenue et revitalisée par le renversement de ces conceptions du pouvoir, en les remplaçant par le pouvoir du service (diaconie). Ce service est véritablement unificateur s'il ne déresponsabilise pas ou ne remplace pas la capacité d'action de celles et ceux qui le reçoivent. La diaconie, qui sert l'unité de l'Église, est menée dans l'amour, l'amour sacrificiel. Cet amour doit surpasser l'amour maternel

---

13 Mary Jane Gorman, *Watching the Disciples: Learning from Their Mistakes*, (Nashville, TN: Abingdon Press, 2008), https://books.google.co.za/books?id=-ax0qIW55nkC&pg.

pour les deux fils. C'est cet amour avec lequel Dieu a aimé toute l'humanité. Il s'agit d'un amour qui transcende les alliances patriarcales et matriarcales, mais qui construit de nouvelles affiliations d'amour entre frères et sœurs dans la famille de Dieu. Il s'agit d'un amour qui surpasse les alliances idéologiques conçues pour protéger les privilèges de quelques-un-e-s. Ce véritable amour élargit le cercle pour inclure celles et ceux qui seraient normalement disqualifié-e-s. Un tel amour fait tomber les murs de la bigoterie et de la fierté raciales et ethniques. Il s'agit d'un amour qui rend humble sans humilier.

Dans l'humilité, cet amour s'exprime par le service autosacrificiel d'un esclave, le *doulos*. L'amour qui adopte ce type de service ne repose pas sur des sentiments érotiques et passionnels. Il n'est pas simplement filial ni fondé sur l'amitié. Il n'est pas nécessairement fondé sur l'amour des parents pour les enfants ou l'amour des proches. Sa source doit être l'amour agape, l'amour de celles et ceux qui sont créé-e-s à l'image de Dieu. Il s'agit de l'amour de Dieu partagé avec nous en Jésus-Christ. C'est cet amour qui peut enlever le poison des formes oppressives de pouvoir dans l'Église et dans le monde.

L'Église animée par cet amour est un témoignage puissant dans le monde, car elle offre une autre façon d'exercer le pouvoir. L'exercice du pouvoir par l'Église ne peut pas refléter celui du monde. Il doit être le sel et la lumière du monde. L'Église contribue à la transformation des dispositions déséquilibrées en matière de pouvoir dans le monde par le témoignage de ses membres, qui vivent dans la société en tant que représentants du Royaume de Dieu à venir. Par leur vie exemplaire et leurs paroles, dans leur famille, dans leur communauté, dans l'Église et dans la sphère publique, celles-ci et ceux-ci s'imposent aux portes de l'Hadès.

L'Église témoigne également au monde lorsqu'elle prend sans équivoque des positions qui sont parfois impopulaires et dangereuses. Jésus déclare: «Quand vous parlez, dites "Oui" ou "Non": tout le reste vient du Malin» (Matthieu 5,37). Le témoignage courageux et sacrificiel de l'Église vise à saper et, en fin de compte, à déraciner tous les systèmes qui génèrent des relations de pouvoir injustes et inégales dans le monde et dans l'Église et à y résister. Les Églises fidèles doivent pouvoir dire: «Cela ne sera pas ainsi parmi nous!» Les Églises tiendront ces propos aux niveaux local, régional, national et mondial. L'Église doit dire «non» au militarisme croissant, aux marchés non productifs, au matérialisme, au monoculturalisme, à la manipulation, à la désinformation, à la malveillance, à la justice populaire et au monopole croissant sur le public et les biens communs. Dans la même veine, l'Église criera un «OUI!» emphatique. Elle dit oui à la miséricorde et à la compassion, à des relations sérieuses, à la coopération multilatérale des nations, à des solutions de médiation aux conflits, à la modération des positions et à la mutualité. C'est la réorganisation du pouvoir à laquelle Jésus nous appelle!

CONTRIBUTIONS

La pasteure **Hyunju Bae** est une ancienne professeure de l'Université presbytérienne de Busan, en République de Corée, et a été ministre ordonnée de l'Église presbytérienne de Corée. Elle a été membre du Comité exécutif et du Comité central du Conseil œcuménique des Églises pour la période allant de Busan à Karlsruhe. Elle est coprésidente du Korea Christian Environmental Movement Solidarity for Integrity of Creation.

L'Archimandrite **Jack Khalil** du Patriarcat grec orthodoxe d'Antioche et de tout l'Orient. Doyen de l'Institut de théologie Saint-Jean de Damas (Syrie), Université de Balamand, et professeur d'études du Nouveau Testament, il est titulaire d'un doctorat de l'Université Aristote de Thessalonique et a étudié pendant trois ans en tant que chercheur invité à l'Eberhard-Karls-Universität de Tübingen, en Allemagne. Il est membre du Comité central du COE et de la Commission Foi et Constitution.

Krzysztof Mielcarek est théologien, bibliste et professeur associé de la faculté de théologie de l'Université catholique Jean-Paul II de Lublin (Pologne). Il est l'un des rédacteurs et traducteurs de la Bible œcuménique polonaise (2017). Il est commissaire catholique romain au sein de la Commission Foi et Constitution du Conseil œcuménique des Églises depuis 2014.

Le pasteur **Kenneth Mtata** est un théologien zimbabwéen et le secrétaire général du Conseil des Églises du Zimbabwe. Il a travaillé dans le domaine de l'herméneutique, l'Église dans l'engagement public, et l'interface entre la religion et la transformation sociale. Son doctorat à l'Université de KwaZulu-Natal portait sur l'espace et le lieu dans l'Évangile selon Jean.

Diana Tsaghikyan est professeure adjointe à la faculté de théologie de l'université d'État d'Erevan (Arménie), et responsable du programme de premier cycle. Elle est également membre du comité de thèse de doctorat au séminaire théologique Gevorkian (université), Mère-Siège de Saint Etchmiadzin. Diana Tsaghikyan a rejoint le COE en 2019 en tant que représentante de l'Église apostolique arménienne (Mère-Siège de Saint Etchmiadzin) et membre du Comité central. Elle a obtenu son doctorat et sa maîtrise en théologie à l'Université d'Édimbourg (Écosse), une maîtrise en études religieuses au Central Baptist Theological Seminary de KS aux États-Unis et une licence à l'Université d'État des langues et des sciences sociales d'Erevan. Ses principales recherches portent sur les études patristiques et la doctrine chrétienne. Elle s'intéresse particulièrement à la littérature théologique des pères de l'Église arménienne. Ses autres intérêts de recherche comprennent les études œcuméniques et les questions contemporaines en théologie.

Paulo Ueti est un Brésilien de mère japonaise et de père italien. Il étudie les théologies latino-américaines, les études bibliques contextuelles, le canon du Nouveau Testament et sa relation avec l'histoire de l'Église et les théologies de l'empire, la spiritualité, le genre, la justice environnementale et l'ecclésiologie. Il est membre du Centre œcuménique d'études bibliques (CEBI) de l'Église anglicane épiscopale du Brésil et travaille à Londres au Bureau de la Communion anglicane avec l'Alliance anglicane (agence de développement, d'aide et de défense) et le Département de l'éducation théologique.

ÍNDICE

INTRODUCCIÓN

Los estudios bíblicos por los sesiones plenarias temáticas son un aspecto importante del trabajo de la asamblea. Dan a los participantes la oportunidad de reunirse diariamente en torno a un pasaje de la Biblia para reflexionar sobre el tema y sobre la experiencia de la asamblea. Los y las participantes pueden discernir conjuntamente los propósitos de Dios para ellos mismos y para el movimiento ecuménico. Se reúnen en grupos lo suficientemente pequeños para permitir que todos contribuyan y lo suficientemente grandes para aportar una variedad de perspectivas.

Las sesiones de estudio bíblico dan a los participantes la oportunidad de explorar juntos el tema de la asamblea a la luz de los textos, el conocimiento y la experiencia de la Biblia. Involucrarse en un estudio bíblico grupal es estar abiertos a los demás, al pasaje de la Biblia y al Espíritu Santo. No se trata de ganar un argumento o persuadir a los demás de un punto de vista en particular. Estas sesiones deben ser un lugar donde los y las participantes puedan integrar todo lo que han escuchado y hecho en la asamblea y descubrir conjuntamente las posibilidades de transformación que Dios nos ofrece.

PROGRAMA

Día 2, jueves, 1 de septiembre de 2022

Tema del día: *El propósito del amor de Dios en Cristo por toda la creación: Reconciliación y unidad*
Referencia bíblica: Col 1:19s (Ef. 1:10) y Mat. 9:35s (La compasión de Cristo)
Tema de la sesión plenaria: *El propósito del amor de Dios encarnado en Jesucristo: Reconciliación y unidad*
Reflexión de: P. Jack Khalil y Revda. Dra. Hyunju Bae

Día 3, viernes, 2 de septiembre de 2022

Tema del día: *Europa*
Referencia bíblica: Lucas 10:25-37 (El buen samaritano)
Tema de la sesión plenaria: ***Europa***
Reflexión de: Dr. Prof. Krzysztof Mielcarek (Polonia/Europa)

Día 6, lunes, 5 de septiembre de 2022

Tema del día: El amor de Cristo: Compasión por la vida
Referencia bíblica: Juan 9:1-12
Tema de la sesión plenaria: *Afirmar la plenitud de la vida*
Reflexión de: Dra. Profa. Diana Tsaghikyan (Europa)
Día 7, martes, 6 de septiembre de 2022
Tema del día: *El amor de Cristo: Transformar el discipulado*
Referencia bíblica: Mateo 15:21-28 (La mujer cananea)
Tema de la sesión plenaria: *Afirmar la justicia y la dignidad humana*
Reflexión de: Dr. Paolo Ueti (Brasil/Sudamérica)

Día 8, miércoles, 7 de septiembre de 2022

Tema del día: *El amor de Cristo: El vínculo entre la unidad cristiana y el testimonio común de las iglesias*
Referencia bíblica: Mateo 20:20-28
Tema de la sesión plenaria tématica: *La unidad cristiana y el testimonio común de las iglesias*
Reflexión de: Rev. Dr. Kenneth Mtata (Zimbabue/África)

Oremos unos por otros en preparación para esta actividad y para participar en la Asamblea. Dejemos que *el amor de Cristo lleve al mundo a la reconciliación y la unidad.*

EL PROPÓSITO DEL AMOR DE DIOS EN CRISTO POR TODA LA CREACIÓN: RECONCILIACIÓN Y UNIDAD

Jack Khalil

> [19] *Por cuanto agradó al Padre que en él habitara toda plenitud* [20] *y, por medio de él, reconciliar consigo mismo todas las cosas, tanto sobre la tierra como en los cielos, habiendo hecho la paz mediante la sangre de su cruz.*
> **—Colosenses 1:19–20**

Estos versos están escritos en el himno cristológico de Colosenses 1:15-20. Ya sea que vengan de un himno tradicional más antiguo o que hayan sido escritos por Pablo mismo en forma de himno, este pasaje es como música para los oídos de quienes aman a Dios. Establece una relación entre la economía divina de la salvación y la teología de la creación, identificando al Redentor del mundo como el Creador que dio existencia a todas las cosas. La primera estrofa (vv. 15-18a) revela la identidad de Cristo como creador de todas las cosas "en los cielos y en la tierra" (v. 16) y concluye con un giro hacia Cristo mismo como cabeza de la iglesia (v. 18a). La segunda estrofa (vv. 18b-20) expone la beneficencia de Cristo hacia todas las cosas "tanto sobre la tierra como en los cielos" (v. 20), como lo demuestra su encarnación (v. 19), su pasión, su muerte y su resurrección por todos los humanos. Se expone claramente que los eventos históricos que se mencionan en la segunda estrofa están íntimamente relacionados con lo que afirma la primera; es decir, que Cristo es el creador de todas las cosas y que el amor de Cristo, que se manifiesta a través de la reconciliación de todas las cosas consigo mismo a través de Su sangre, está arraigado en el amor que muestra en la creación de todas las cosas. La repetición de "todas las cosas… en los cielos y en la tierra" –tanto en la primera estrofa, que habla de la creación, como en la segunda estrofa, que habla de su reconciliación– valida el comentario anterior que propone que la reconciliación de todas las cosas viene del amor de Cristo por todas las cosas que ha creado. El amor de Cristo es un amor desde la eternidad por la eternidad. Él cuida y guarda todas las cosas en el cielo y en la tierra, porque son suyas.

El amor de Cristo nos llama y nos lleva a la reconciliación. Nos llama a arrepentirnos por nuestra enemistad con Él (v. 21) que mostramos haciendo el mal al prójimo y a Su universo. Es útil tener conciencia de que nuestro pecado contra Dios no se reduce a la blasfemia y la ingratitud, sino que es primeramente un pecado humanamente relacional y ecológico.

Según Romanos 8:7, la enemistad es una consecuencia de "la intención de la carne". Esto quiere decir que la fuente de la enemistad es tratar de complacerse a sí mismo y satisfacer los propios deseos egoístas (Gal. 5:16) en perjuicio de los demás seres humanos. La "idolatría, hechicería, enemistades, pleitos, celos, ira, contiendas, disensiones, partidismos," (Gal. 5:2) como deseos de naturaleza pecaminosa son ejemplos representativos de pecados relacionales. En este sentido, Colosenses 1:21 dice que la enemistad de los humanos hacia Dios existe debido a su actitud y sus malas acciones.

El hecho de que el pecado y las malas acciones

enemisten a los humanos con Dios no quiere decir que el pecado traiga consigo una enemistad mutua entre Dios y la humanidad, ni que Dios sea hostil con los pecadores. Esta visión no aparece en ninguna de las epístolas de San Pablo. En cambio, Pablo esclarece, sin lugar a dudas, de quién y hacia quién existe la hostilidad cuando señala que "la intención de la carne es enemistad contra Dios" (Rom. 8:7) y que la enemistad existe por la actitud y las malas obras de los humanos (Col. 1:21).

San Juan Crisóstomo señala más precisamente: "¿Y qué ruega él? '¿Ser reconciliados con Dios?' Y él dijo que no. 'Reconcíliense con Dios mismo', porque no es él quien se enemista, sino ustedes, porque Dios nunca es hostil". [1] De hecho, tanto la voz activa, "reconciliar" (καταλλάξαι o ἀποκαταλλάξαι), usada en Colosenses 1:20 y dondequiera que Pablo habla de la obra de Dios, y la voz pasiva, "ser reconciliado" (καταλλάττεσθαι), usada cuando Pablo exhorta a los cristianos a reconciliarse con Dios, muestran sin lugar a dudas que Dios nos ha reconciliado consigo mismo.

Dios reconcilia a quienes se convirtieron en sus enemigos y a quienes le mostraron ingratitud al contribuir a los conflictos y guerras, a las desigualdades sociales y económicas, a la crisis climática y a la pandemia de la COVID-19. El perdón de la enemistad a través de la muerte y la resurrección de Cristo ofreció la paz a todos los humanos que se hicieron enemigos con estos actos pecaminosos.

Solo el Hijo encarnado, "por cuanto agradó al Padre que en él habitara toda plenitud" (Col. 1:19), puede restaurar la paz donde reina la enemistad, volver a instituir la justicia donde muchos sufren injusticias y reinstituir la unidad entre quienes están oscurecidos por la "idolatría, hechicería, enemistades, pleitos, celos, ira, contiendas, disensiones, partidismos".

Los seres humanos nunca hubieran podido alcanzar por sí mismos la rectitud necesaria para reconciliarse con Dios. Sabiendo esto, el apóstol Pablo, en el versículo 20, conecta el momento de la reconciliación con la muerte de Cristo en la cruz ("mediante la sangre que derramó en la cruz").

La sangre divina, derramada en la cruz por nosotros, por su poder para perdonar la enemistad, hizo la paz con todas las cosas "en el cielo o en la tierra". De la misma manera, la muerte y resurrección salvadora de Cristo trae la unidad a todos los que se conmovieron por su amor. Aquellos que repudiaron el amor egoísta, que es la raíz del pecado, y aprendieron del amor y la entrega abnegada de Cristo, serán reconciliados a través de Cristo, incluso los unos con los otros. Ellos responderán a la bondad y la compasión de Cristo aceptando el amor, la justicia y la paz como dogmas del comportamiento hacia "todas las cosas" y todos los humanos, que Cristo ama y por quienes murió.

Hoy estamos llamados juntos a expresar gratitud por el amor de Cristo por nuestro mundo y por todos los seres humanos, y a reflexionar en oración y arrepentimiento sobre nuestra respuesta tangible a su amor. Tenemos la intención, con todo nuestro corazón, de aprender de la sangre de la cruz que todos tenemos que hacer sacrificios y emprender acciones comunes por la justicia, la paz y la reconciliación a través de Cristo, nuestro santo Señor de gloria.

1. ¿Cómo nos lleva el amor de Cristo a la justicia y la unidad? ¿Qué aprendemos de Su amor?
2. ¿Cómo podemos mostrar gratitud en respuesta al amor de Dios? ¿Cuáles son las acciones tangibles que Dios nos impulsa a

1 San Juan Crisostomo, "Homilias sobre 2 Corintios", en New Advent, https://www.newadvent.org/fathers/2202.htm [Inglés]

emprender respecto a los seres humanos y
a toda la creación?

EL PROPÓSITO DEL AMOR DE DIOS EN CRISTO POR TODA LA CREACIÓN: RECONCILIACIÓN Y UNIDAD

Hyunju Bae

35 Jesús recorría todas las ciudades y las aldeas, enseñando en sus sinagogas, predicando el evangelio del reino y sanando toda enfermedad y toda dolencia. 36 Y cuando vio las multitudes, tuvo compasión de ellas porque estaban acosadas y desamparadas como ovejas que no tienen pastor. 37 Entonces dijo a sus discípulos: "A la verdad, la mies es mucha, pero los obreros son pocos. 38 Rueguen, pues, al Señor de la mies, que envíe obreros a su mies".
—Mateo 9:35–38

Jesús compasivo

Mateo 9:35–38 es una encrucijada. Recuerda el ministerio de Jesús y anticipa sus enseñanzas sobre la misión de los discípulos. El versículo 35 resume las acciones de Jesús descritas en Mateo 4:23 repitiendo palabras tales como *enseñar*, *predicar* y *sanar*. A estas actividades se les llama *ministerio tripartito de Jesús*. Jesús iluminó las mentes de las personas, las invitó a abrir sus corazones al advenimiento del reino de Dios, y sanó sus padecimientos físicos.

El versículo 36 revela que la compasión es la fuerza que impulsa el ministerio de Jesús. Jesús tuvo compasión por las personas acosadas y desamparadas. "Acosado" (*eskylmenoi*) originalmente significaba ser desollado o despellejado. "Desamparado" (*errimmenoi*) significa estar postrado o yacer en el suelo. Las personas eran explotadas, desmoralizadas, agotadas, oprimidas y aplastadas. El verbo *splagchnizomai [tener compasión]*, en griego, que se usa en Mateo para describir la compasión de Jesús (14:14; 15:32; 18:27; 20:34), se deriva del sustantivo *splagchnon*, y tiene los siguientes significados: primero, las partes internas del cuerpo, o las entrañas; segundo, el corazón; tercero, amor o afecto. La compasión que Jesús mostró en sus actos de misericordia (5:7; 9:13) fluye espontáneamente de la capacidad del amor para sentir y tener empatía desde las entrañas; es decir, de una manera holística que integra el corazón y el cuerpo. La compasión es el principal creador del ministerio tripartito de Jesús.

En Mateo 9:37, Jesús revela su sentido de la realidad al reconocer el desequilibrio entre la cosecha [mies] abundante y la escasez de obreros. Esto no lleva a la desesperanza, sino a la oración y al reconocimiento de la gran oportunidad. En el versículo siguiente, Jesús exhorta a sus discípulos a orar para que el Señor de la cosecha [la mies] mande obreros a su campo. Esta sección prepara el terreno para la enseñanza de Jesús sobre el discipulado y la misión en el capítulo 10.

Jesús de Nazaret vivió con un corazón de compasión profunda y visceral. La parábola de Jesús del hombre rico que vive con un corazón de piedra captura un claro contraste con este corazón compasivo. El hombre rico que "se vestía de púrpura y de lino fino, y hacía cada día banquete con esplendidez", era apático y ciego a las necesidades de Lázaro, un hombre pobre que se echaba a la puerta de su casa, "estaba echado a su puerta, lleno de llagas, y deseaba saciarse con lo que caía de la mesa del rico. Aun los perros venían y le lamían las llagas" (Lucas 16:19-21). El hombre rico no pudo ver a Lázaro, su prójimo, que vivía en una miseria deshumanizante, porque su corazón era rígido, duro y egocéntrico. Al monopolizar la abundancia de posesiones, no promueve la vida en los demás. Esclavizado por la avaricia, no comprende la sabiduría de Jesús: "— Miren, guárdense de toda codicia, porque la vida de uno no consiste en la abundancia de los bienes que posee" (Lucas 12:15). Mientras que Lázaro era visto como menos que un ser humano por su condición física, el hombre rico estaba mucho más deshumanizado por su falta de conciencia y su falta de sensibilidad con el prójimo. El corazón compasivo nos evita caer en la trampa de la avaricia o escondernos detrás del mundo de la dualidad, la abstracción y el cálculo. La compasión es el centro del amor de Cristo y la luz que nos guía para convertirnos en "imitadores de Dios" (Ef. 5:1). "Sean misericordiosos, como también su Padre es misericordioso" (Lucas 6:36).

Los signos del Antropoceno nos dicen que la humanidad no tiene futuro si no hacemos un esfuerzo conjunto para construir una civilización compasiva. Nuestra compasión necesita estar dirigida tanto a las personas como a la naturaleza. Un corazón humano cruel e insensible al resto de los humanos no se convertirá en un corazón eco-sensible de un día para otro. Como el arzobispo Desmond Tutu dijo, "Una vez que empezamos a vivir de una manera amigable con las personas con toda la familia de Dios, también seremos amigables con el medio ambiente".[2] La fe cristiana auténtica puede facilitar este proceso porque se centra en Jesús, que ha traído la paz a la tierra que nos reconcilia con Dios, con los demás, y con toda la creación de Dios (Ef. 1:10; Col. 1:15-20). Jesús dijo "He venido a echar fuego en la tierra. ¡Y cómo quisiera que ya estuviera encendido!" (Lucas 12:49). El fuego de compasión, que fomenta el poder relacional de las personas, es la base de una nueva civilización que celebra el tejido de la vida y la convivialidad, porque puede dar forma a una contracultura amigable con los seres humanos y con la naturaleza.

La compasión es la calidad del liderazgo. La referencia a las "ovejas que no tienen pastor" (Mateo 9:36) evoca el mal gobierno de pastores falsos que son líderes infieles. Se hace eco de Ezequiel 34, que condena a los falsos pastores de Israel. Ellos dañan a las ovejas al no fortalecer a las débiles, no curar a las enfermas, no vendar las perniquebradas, no hacer que vuelvan las descarriadas ni buscar a las perdidas. Dominan a las personas con dureza y con violencia (Ezq. 34:4). Los falsos pastores nunca buscan o van por las ovejas descarriadas para evitar que estén a merced de las fieras salvajes (Ezequiel 34:5-8). Jesús, el pastor verdadero de su pueblo (Mateo 2:6) es diferente. El primer verbo de Mateo 9:35 indica que Jesús "recorría" todas las ciudades y aldeas (como se dijo antes, en 4:23). Este verbo es la traducción del pretérito imperfecto del verbo *periagō* en griego, y se refiere a la acción que Jesús realizó repetidamente o durante un tiempo continuado. Jesús no llevó una vida indiferente y egocéntrica. Buscó relacionarse con las personas en la tierra para ver su situación con sus propios ojos. "He aquí, yo mismo buscaré mis ovejas y cuidaré de ellas". (Ezequiel 34:11). Jesús es un pastor davídico (Ezequiel 34:23) y el verdadero líder enviado por Dios.

La declaración del Comité Ejecutivo del CMI de noviembre de 2021 sobre el resultado de la COP26 insta "a todas las iglesias miembros, a los asociados ecuménicos y a las comunidades cristianas a que sean líderes, y no solo seguidores, en la realización de los cambios por los que

---

2 Arzobispo Desmond Tutu, "Prólogo" en *The Green Bible*, (San Francisco: Harper Bibles, 2010), I-13 [Inglés].

abogamos".[3] Cuando se necesita urgentemente el ejercicio del liderazgo a todos los niveles de nuestras comunidades, en la familia, en la iglesia y en la sociedad, la calidad del liderazgo es importante. El liderazgo debe expeditar la *metanoia* en toda la civilización e incentivar la participación de todos. "La creación aguarda con ardiente anhelo la manifestación de los hijos de Dios" (Rom. 8:19). El mundo ahora espera las contribuciones activas y diversas de personas despiertas de todas las esferas, cuya motivación venga de la conciencia y que tengan el valor de cambiar. En consonancia con el exhorto de Jesús, pedimos a Dios que mande más obreros para expandir el acuciante ministerio de sanación, restauración, reconciliación y unidad para transformar nuestro mundo herido. Como discípulos de Jesús, estamos convocados a responder a un llamado urgente para revitalizar el ministerio y la misión, llenos del fuego de la compasión que se enciende con el movimiento de Jesús. Para responder al llamado, "queremos avanzar unidos".[4] Continuaremos orando, trabajando y avanzando juntos en nuestro deseo de dar a conocer al mundo la presencia de Dios, el Emanuel entre nosotros. (Mat. 1:23).

3 Comité Ejecutivo del CMI, "Declaración de Resultados de la COP26", del 16 de noviembre de 2021, https://www.oikoumene.org/es/resources/documents/statement-on-the-outcome-of-cop26.

4 Mensaje de la 1.ª Asamblea del Consejo Mundial de Iglesias en Ámsterdam, Países Bajos, 1948. En la 10.ª asamblea, se presentó una invitación a una peregrinación de justicia y paz con la frase "Queremos avanzar unidos". ("Mensaje de la 10. ª Asamblea del CMI", Busan, República de Corea, del 30 de octubre al 8 de noviembre de 2013, https://www.oikoumene.org/es/resources/documents/message-of-the-wcc-10th-assembly.

EL AMOR DE CRISTO LLEVA AL MUNDO A LA RECONCILIACIÓN Y LA UNIDAD

Krzysztof Mielcarek

[25] Y he aquí, cierto maestro de la ley se levantó para probarle, diciendo: "Maestro, ¿haciendo qué cosa poseeré la vida eterna?" [26] Y él le dijo: "¿Qué está escrito en la ley? ¿Cómo lees?" [27] Él le respondió diciendo: "Amarás al Señor tu Dios con todo tu corazón, con toda tu alma, con todas tus fuerzas y con toda tu mente; y a tu prójimo como a ti mismo". [28] Le dijo: "Has respondido bien. Haz esto y vivirás". [29] Pero él, queriendo justificarse, le preguntó a Jesús: "¿Y quién es mi prójimo?" [30] Respondiendo Jesús, le dijo: "Cierto hombre descendía de Jerusalén a Jericó, y cayó en manos de ladrones quienes lo despojaron de su ropa, lo hirieron y se fueron dejándolo medio muerto. [31] Por casualidad, descendía cierto sacerdote por aquel camino y, al verle, pasó de largo. [32] De igual manera, un levita también llegó al lugar y, al ir y verle, pasó de largo. [33] Pero cierto samaritano, que iba de viaje, llegó cerca de él y, al verle, fue movido a misericordia. [34] Acercándose a él, vendó sus heridas echándoles aceite y vino. Y poniéndolo sobre su propia cabalgadura, lo llevó a un mesón y cuidó de él. [35] Al día siguiente sacó dos monedas y se las dio al mesonero diciéndole: 'Cuídamelo, y todo lo que gastes de más yo te lo pagaré cuando vuelva'. [36] ¿Cuál de estos tres te parece haber sido el prójimo de aquel que cayó en manos de ladrones?" [37] Él dijo: "El que hizo misericordia con él". Entonces Jesús le dijo: "Ve y haz tú lo mismo".

—Lucas 10:25–37

"¿Haciendo qué cosas poseeré la vida eterna?" "¿Qué está escrito en la ley? ¿Cómo lees?" El diálogo preliminar de Jesús con el maestro la ley nos lleva al núcleo de la perícopa que acabamos de leer. Ya que la vida eterna depende de nuestro amor a Dios y al prójimo, para los cristianos no existe asunto más importante que este compromiso. Cada israelita devoto recuerda esta verdad fundamental recitando Shemá Israel cada día. Sin embargo, el maestro de la ley lleva el diálogo a otro nivel al pedirle a Jesús que identifique los objetos de su amor. No existe dificultad con el primero, porque es Dios. Pero ¿quién es el prójimo? Esta pregunta es el centro de la parábola que Jesús cita y que está entrelazada con su protagonista.

Aunque la tradición bíblica ha llamado a esta historia la "parábola del buen samaritano", la figura que une a sus héroes no es un samaritano, sino un hombre pobre que, cuando descendía de Jerusalén hacia Jericó, es atacado por ladrones. La parábola comienza con él, y él está presente hasta el final. A pesar de que el narrador no nos cuenta esta historia desde su perspectiva, el hombre pobre está en el centro de la parábola. Es él quien puede ser identificado como el prójimo sobre el que pregunta el maestro de la ley. Para parafrasear otras parábolas del maestro de Nazaret, se podría decir que cada prójimo necesitado es como un hombre atacado por ladrones.

Al darle esta interpretación a "prójimo", Jesús expande conscientemente el concepto bíblico del término *rēʿa*, en hebreo, o del término *plesíon,* en griego, que usualmente significaba amigo o vecino. Sin embargo, la historia no dice que el sacerdote, el levita, o el samaritano conocieran a la víctima con anterioridad. Por lo tanto, el personaje principal de la parábola cumple todos los criterios para ser un extraño.[5] De hecho, la construcción de la parábola fortalece gradualmente la distancia entre la persona atacada y las tres personas que pasaban por ahí, porque el versículo 30 sugiere que era un peregrino judío que regresaba a casa tras visitar el Santuario en Jerusalén. Esto deja entrever que había al menos alguna clase de vínculo formal entre él y el personal del templo. Pero ambos lo vieron en el camino y no solo siguieron de largo, sino que también se desviaron (*antiparerchomai*) para no acercarse más a la víctima del asalto. Así, aumentan su distancia con el necesitado.[6]

Por otro lado, el samaritano es la personificación de la extrañeza del hombre atacado.[7] Este último, que probablemente era un judío devoto, hubiera tratado a todos los samaritanos como renegados.[8] El odio era mutuo. Por lo tanto, podemos afirmar que hay una distancia extrema entre los personajes. Sin embargo, el samaritano cruza la barrera de la hostilidad y el resentimiento.

La parábola de Jesús centra la atención del oyente en las acciones del samaritano. Este ve a un hombre necesitado y se conmueve por su situación. Pero la compasión del samaritano no es una emoción vacía porque toma acciones concretas. Se acerca a la víctima, cura sus heridas, lo lleva a un alojamiento, lo cuida y paga dinero para cubrir los costos adicionales de su recuperación. Cabe señalar que Jesús no comparte con sus oyentes el posible final feliz de la historia, sino que los deja con cierta duda. De este modo, su atención se centra completamente en la actitud del samaritano hacia la víctima; es decir, que hizo todo lo que pudo para cuidar de este hombre.

La frase "todo lo que pudo" requiere un breve comentario: la yuxtaposición del samaritano con Jesús lleva a muchos predicadores a exagerar su actitud compasiva como devoción total. Sin embargo, vale la pena señalar que el epílogo de la parábola presenta una imagen distinta. El samaritano finalmente reanuda sus actividades diarias y deja al atacado al cuidado del dueño del mesón (10:35). No somete su vida entera a la víctima del robo, pero apoya al hombre según sus necesidades.

¿Cuáles son las consecuencias del mensaje de Jesús para los cristianos y cristianas de hoy? Estas pueden expresarse en varios puntos:

1. Puede encontrarse frente a una situación en la que su prójimo necesite ayuda repentinamente.
2. Pertenecer a instituciones religiosas no garantiza una actitud apropiada hacia los necesitados.

---

5 Hebreo: *ben-nēḵar/'iš-noḵri/gēr/zār*; Griego: *allótrios/allogenēs/ pároikos*. Ver Génesis 17:12–27; 42:7; Ester 8:12; 1 Miqueas 12:10; Job 28:4; Salmos 35:15; 105:12; 109:11; Proverbios 5:10; 8:8; 14:10; 27:2; Eclesiastés. 6:2; Sirácides 32:18; Isaías 61:5; Jeremías 14:8; 51:51; Oseas 7:9; 8:7; Joel 4:17; Abdías 1:11; y Efesios 2:12; 4:18.

6 Algunos ven en la actitud del sacerdote y el levita el deseo de evitar la contaminación ritual, mientras otros ven en ella su asco por el hombre golpeado.

7 Los comentadores señalan que el contenido de esta parábola debió impactar a los oyentes de Jesús. Hay otros ejemplos de esto en el Evangelio de Lucas. Consulte, por ejemplo, la limpieza de los leprosos por parte de Jesús (Lucas 17:11-19).

8 Los orígenes del pueblo samaritano se asocian con la conquista de Israel por los Asirios (722 a. de C.). Por tanto, parte de la población del reino fue trasladada a Mesopotamia y, en su lugar, se estableció una población extranjera con una cultura y creencias diferentes (2 Reyes 17:24-41). Con el tiempo se integraron y sus creencias se fusionaron con las de los israelitas. Esto dio lugar a una religión ecléctica con su centro en la cima del Monte Guerizín. Las diferencias entre los judíos y los samaritanos causaron resentimiento mutuo (ver Juan 4:9, *Talmud Jerušalaim: Shekalim* 1.4.3; *Shevi'it* 6.1.16; 8.8.1).

3. Actúe según lo que es bueno y justo, sin importar los prejuicios negativos de los demás.
4. Ayude a quien lo necesite, incluso si esto lo/a priva a usted de su comodidad, sus posesiones o su tiempo.
5. Actúe de manera adecuada para satisfacer las necesidades de su prójimo.

El mundo moderno no nos permite estudiar esta parábola solo desde el punto de vista de un solo hombre. Hoy, naciones enteras e incluso continentes están sufriendo, y esto requiere una respuesta global y sistémica. Se han establecido muchas religiones y organizaciones internacionales para ayudar a las víctimas de nuestros tiempos. Las enormes desigualdades en la riqueza y el nivel de vida han causado oleadas migratorias de personas que buscan mejores condiciones de vida. Una serie de conflictos regionales sangrientos han expulsado a muchos refugiados de sus hogares. Por lo tanto, los países y las regiones prósperos deben tomar medidas intencionadas para mitigar la miseria de las víctimas de estos fenómenos desastrosos. En las décadas recientes hemos visto ejemplos sin precedentes de generosidad heroica y de fría indiferencia. Debemos, entonces, orar por que la comunidad internacional aprenda de sus errores y emprenda acciones efectivas. Las iglesias individuales, especialmente aquellas que tienen un alcance global, también tienen un papel importante.

Sin embargo, todos deberíamos tomar como punto de partida el preguntarnos: ¿Hasta qué punto soy el prójimo de otra persona? ¿Hasta qué punto me estoy comportando como su prójimo? La parábola de Jesús es una suerte de clamor, un llamado para que seamos el prójimo, aunque signifique renunciar a una parte de nuestra comodidad, nuestras posesiones o nuestro tiempo.

La respuesta de Jesús a la pregunta del maestro de la ley es, de hecho, "TODOS". El discípulo de Cristo está, entonces, llamado a romper barreras religiosas, culturales y políticas y a llegar a los necesitados. El tema de esta asamblea, "El amor de Cristo lleva al mundo a la reconciliación y la unidad", puede reformularse de la siguiente manera: "La misericordia de Cristo nos lleva a descubrir a nuestro prójimo en cada ser humano".

EL AMOR DE CRISTO –COMPASIÓN POR LA VIDA– AFIRMAR LA PLENITUD DE LA VIDA

Diana Tsaghikyan

[1]Mientras pasaba Jesús, vio a un hombre ciego de nacimiento, [2] y sus discípulos le preguntaron diciendo: "Rabí, ¿quién pecó, este o sus padres, para que naciera ciego?" [3] Respondió Jesús: "No es que este pecó, ni tampoco sus padres. Al contrario, fue para que las obras de Dios se manifestaran en él. [4] Me es preciso hacer las obras del que me envió mientras dure el día. La noche viene cuando nadie puede trabajar. [5] Mientras yo esté en el mundo, luz soy del mundo". [6] Dicho esto, escupió en tierra, hizo lodo con la saliva y con el lodo untó los ojos del ciego. [7] Y le dijo: "Ve, lávate en el estanque de Siloé (que significa enviado)". Por tanto fue, se lavó y regresó viendo. [8] Entonces los vecinos y los que antes lo habían visto que era mendigo decían: "¿No es este el que se sentaba para mendigar?" [9] Unos decían: "Este es". Y otros: "No. Pero se parece a él". Él decía: "Yo soy". [10] Entonces le decían: "¿Cómo te fueron abiertos los ojos?" [11] Él respondió: "El hombre que se llama Jesús hizo lodo, me untó los ojos y me dijo: 'Ve a Siloé y lávate'. Entonces, cuando fui y me lavé, recibí la vista". [12] Y le dijeron: "¿Dónde está él?" Él dijo: "No sé".
—Juan 9:1–12

Las personas consideran que la sanación del hombre ciego es un milagro. Jesús vio a un hombre ciego y, maravillosamente, le permitió ver. En efecto, la sanación del hombre ciego fue un milagro. Los milagros sucedieron entonces y suceden de muchas maneras también ahora. Sin embargo, esta historia no solo se trata de un milagro, sino también del amor de Cristo y del poder de la compasión.

¿Qué sabemos del hombre que se sienta a mendigar? Este tenía padres, pero estaba solo; vivía en sociedad, pero estaba excluido de ella. Como era ciego de nacimiento, nunca vio la luz hasta que Cristo lo vio y cambió su realidad. Primero, leímos que Jesús ve a un hombre ciego e inmediatamente somos testigos de la manera en que Jesús rechaza la máxima "Ni el ciego ni el cojo entrará en la casa" (2 Sam. 5:8). Jesús corrige las ideas equivocadas de sus discípulos sobre el pecado y el sufrimiento, los instruye acerca de la obra de Dios y los ilumina declarando: "Mientras yo esté en el mundo, luz soy del mundo". Entonces Jesús hace lodo con su saliva y la unta en los ojos del ciego y dice: "Ve, lávate en el estanque de Siloé". Tras seguir sus instrucciones, al volver, el mendigo ya veía.

Ha ocurrido un milagro increíble, pero nadie parece interesarse ni estar feliz por el hombre que antes estaba ciego. Somos testigos, quizá, de la indiferencia en vez del cuidado y la compasión necesarios. Curiosamente, entre las preguntas que hacen los demás, no encontramos ninguna que intente descubrir las nuevas emociones y sentimientos que ha desarrollado el hombre ciego. Este se encuentra indiferencia en vez de cuidado y compasión. En contraposición, con un amor y gracia puros, Jesús sana al hombre ciego que estaba excluido y marginado. Jesús desafía a la sociedad y actúa. Le da al mendigo un sentimiento profundo de esperanza y una conciencia más profunda del poder salvador de Dios. Restaura la plenitud de la vida del hombre con un nuevo propósito y una nueva dirección. Jesús le da al hombre la visión de la luz.

La decepción, la frustración y la falta de una visión para la vida pueden nublar nuestra vida actual y nuestras esperanzas futuras con la oscuridad de la incertidumbre, pero en tiempos de oscuridad es imperativo que mantengamos una visión de luz. No podemos permanecer en la caverna de la muerte, donde se acalla la inteligencia y no se puede encontrar la devoción o la compasión. Hoy, más que nunca, tras 2022 años, las iglesias cristianas todavía se enfrentan a muchos desafíos. Se necesita una preciada medicina para sanar las heridas del cuerpo de Cristo. La compasión debe ser la respuesta.

La compasión genuina tiene una hermosa relevancia en la manera en la que tratamos a los demás. Tiene el poder de llevar a la humanidad hacia un camino justo donde se aclara el amor de Cristo y se ve la luz. La compasión genuina cambia la manera en que vivimos. Cuando acogemos la compasión en nuestras vidas, intentamos ser clementes, esperanzados, fieles y pacientes. En tiempos de impaciencia, debemos recordar que Dios obra de maneras misteriosas. Debemos valorar que la compasión nos recuerda lo que significa ser humanos.

Cada aspecto de esta historia tiene implicaciones espirituales: provee una figura paralela poderosa al papel que desempeña Dios para llevarnos a la fe y a la salvación a través de la gracia y el poder de la compasión. La compasión es una cualidad fundamental del concepto bíblico de Dios. Jesucristo, en quien Dios "fue manifestado en la carne" (1 Tim. 3:16), es un ejemplo excepcional de compasión. Jesús enseñó que la compasión se debe extender no solo a amigos y a vecinos, sino a todos, sin excepción; a toda la raza humana. Juan el evangelista quiere que restauremos y mantengamos nuestra visión de la luz.

Cada época tiene sus imperativos. En nuestra era materialista y secular, en el contexto de una pandemia mundial, cuando nos enfrentamos a la horrorosa realidad del racismo, la discriminación, la pobreza, la violencia, la inestabilidad política, las guerras y el cambio climático, es imperativo que no nos demos por vencidos. Ahora más que nunca debemos valorar los aspectos espirituales de nuestras vidas. Cada uno de nosotros es único. Tenemos puntos de vista, culturas, experiencias y antecedentes diferentes pero nuestra fe mutua en Cristo y nuestro amor por el Señor nos une. Por sobre todo hay una unidad de servicio y testimonio en todo el mundo en el nombre de Jesucristo, que es "la luz del mundo". La vida no tiene esperanza sin una relación con el Creador y con los demás. Jesucristo abrió un camino amoroso de vida bendita, y este camino luminoso y dador de vida nos hará fuertes y nos dará la seguridad de que cada uno de nosotros tiene un propósito para vivir y crear. Nuestro Señor Jesucristo le dio a la humanidad la esperanza y la gracia para enfrentarse al sufrimiento y heredar la vida eterna.

Creo que, con respeto mutuo y con la firme creencia de que Cristo resucitó, difundiremos la palabra de Dios. Continuaremos buscando humildemente la luz de Dios y trabajando hacia la reconciliación y la unidad. Valoraremos nuestro propósito individual y, habiendo encontrado este propósito, extenderemos un respeto inmenso a nuestra humanidad diversa. Este propósito viene junto con la responsabilidad de actuar con compasión, con el amor de Cristo en nuestras mentes y nuestros corazones y con su luz inquebrantable como guía. Sin embargo, no podemos lograr nada de esto por nuestra cuenta: nos necesitamos unos a otros. Juntos podemos recordar nuestro pasado, vivir nuestro presente y crear nuestro futuro. Tenemos la intención de estar juntos. ¿No es esto un milagro?

> "Luz y fuente de iluminación, que
> vive en luz inaccesible... con la llegada
> de la luz matinal, trae también la luz
> del entendimiento a nuestras almas."9

9 Nerses Shnorhali (San Nerses el Gracioso) fue uno de los teólogos medievales notables y la figura ecuménica por excelencia en la historia de la Iglesia Armenia. Esta cita [traducción libre del inglés] es de su "Himno a la Luz" (Luys ara

EL AMOR DE CRISTO –TRANSFORMAR EL DISCIPULADO– AFIRMAR LA JUSTICIA Y LA DIGNIDAD HUMANA

Paolo Ueti

[21] Cuando Jesús salió de allí, se fue a las regiones de Tiro y de Sidón. [22] Entonces una mujer cananea que había salido de aquellas regiones, clamaba diciendo: "¡Señor, Hijo de David, ten misericordia de mí! Mi hija es gravemente atormentada por un demonio". [23] Pero él no le respondía palabra. Entonces se acercaron sus discípulos y le rogaron diciendo: "Despídela, pues grita tras nosotros". [24] Y respondiendo dijo: "Yo no he sido enviado sino a las ovejas perdidas de la casa de Israel". [25] Entonces ella vino y se postró delante de él diciéndole: "¡Señor, socórreme!" [26] Él le respondió diciendo: "No es bueno tomar el pan de los hijos y echarlo a los perritos". [27] Y ella dijo: "Sí, Señor. Pero aun los perritos comen de las migajas que caen de la mesa de sus dueños". [28] Entonces respondió Jesús y le dijo: "¡Oh mujer, grande es tu fe! Sea hecho contigo como quieres". Y su hija fue sana desde aquella hora.

—Mateo 15:21–28

La versión de Mateo de esta historia, con más elementos que la versión de Marcos 7:24–30, es incluso más provocadora porque incluye a los discípulos de Jesús en la narración. Sabemos que el Evangelio según San Mateo fue escrito alrededor del 80-90 d. de C., y no solo refleja los eventos que sucedieron en los tiempos de Jesús en Palestina, sino también lo que estaba sucediendo en la iglesia de Siria, que probablemente fue el origen de la mayoría de los escritos de esta comunidad.

Este texto trata sobre la comunidad. Se trata de a quiénes acogemos y cómo los acogemos. Y, al tratarse de un texto acerca de la comunidad, presenta una provocación respecto a los hábitos de acogimiento, de reconciliación y de realización de la unidad de Jesucristo. Diferentes personas de distintas culturas, idiomas, antecedentes, hábitos, géneros, edades y posiciones de poder se encuentran en un contexto de violencia de género, racismo, necesidad, dolor, enfermedad, exclusión, xenofobia y prejuicios establecidos.

Sin embargo, siempre es esencial recordarnos que Dios "ama al extranjero" (Deut. 10:18). Cuando leemos el corpus de textos del canon bíblico, nos damos cuenta de que el espíritu de la Torá y de los profetas está muy presente también en el Nuevo Testamento, promoviendo la protección de las personas que se enfrentan a la opresión, la enfermedad, la exclusión y la violencia, que están en desventaja en el sistema y que tienen algún tipo de necesidad que los hace ser percibidos como menos humanos. Los pobres, los extranjeros, los huérfanos, las viudas, los niños, las niñas y las mujeres son algunos de los que deben recibir mayor protección.

El texto desarrolla la metodología dialógica de una mujer extranjera en su encuentro con Jesús, el judío. Ella es cananea y de cultura helénica. Al parecer, su condición de "extranjera" es relevante para el autor de esta historia. Parece haber un problema en la comunidad en cuanto al diálogo, las relaciones y la acogida de los extraños, los extranjeros y las mujeres en la mesa de la comunión. Sabemos que una mesa compartida, *koinonía*, es un lugar para el culto, la celebración y el reconocimiento del caminar de Jesús con nosotros. La mesa compartida nos sana y nos une a todos, o debería hacerlo.

Percibimos el interés del autor de dar el protagonismo a las dos mujeres, la hija y la madre, ambas de nombre desconocido. La situación se presenta como un encuentro, no muy amistoso al inicio, entre dos personas que normalmente no se mirarían a los ojos, y mucho menos conversarían. Para muchas personas de ese tiempo, las personas que no eran judías eran consideradas "perros", de la misma manera que las personas que no eran romanas eran consideradas bárbaros. Sin embargo, este encuentro sucede. Hay un debate, aparentemente entre personas desiguales, pero cuando analizamos el discurso nos damos cuenta de que ambas están al mismo nivel en cuanto a su voluntad de participar, a su técnica y su contenido. La mujer no es completamente sumisa. Es participativa, inteligente, resiliente y persistente para obtener lo que busca.

La conversación se desarrolla por la enfermedad de la hija de la mujer, por sus expectativas de Jesús y por su audacia al interrumpir el deseo de Jesús de no ser descubierto. La mujer confronta a este hombre que no quiere prestar atención a su necesidad y se enfrenta a la grosería y la falta de empatía de los discípulos. Según el texto de Mateo, ella "". Imagine la imagen bochornosa de una mujer gritándole a alguien que quería permanecer en el anonimato. Cuando la mujer lo confronta, Jesús expresa su postura según su tradición cultural, lo que aprendió de niño y la manera en que se crió. Se resiste a compartir el pan y la mesa, que es una metáfora de la comunidad: un grupo de apoyo. Al parecer, la comunidad de Mateo tiene un problema en cuanto a quiénes tienen derecho de acceder a la mesa.

Volviendo a la historia, es interesante observar los problemas que permean el diálogo de estas dos personas de diferentes culturas: un encuentro entre personas desiguales; un espíritu impuro y la necesidad; pan arriba y migas abajo; sobre la mesa y debajo de la mesa. Parecen hablar acerca de temas diferentes y sin relación entre ellos. La mujer, de educación griega, tiene sus necesidades (curar a su hija, expulsar al demonio, recuperar a su hija, obtener ayuda, inscribirse en el universo lingüístico de Jesús). Jesús es intransigente culturalmente (etnocéntrico e intolerante), e intenta impedir el acceso de la mujer a la mesa. En el relato de Mateo, los discípulos le piden a Jesús que la despida, que puede significar "atender" o "despedirla sin atender" pero, sin importar su significado, hay intermediarios molestos por esta relación. En la comunidad de Mateo, parece que la mujer no debería tener derecho de acceder a la mesa, que es Jesús.

La pregunta fundamental de la mujer, desarrollada con propiedad y habilidad retórica, es: ¿Quién tiene acceso a Jesús? ¿Quién puede alcanzar el pan? ¿Solo los hijos de Israel y los pertenecientes al club de Jesús y sus discípulos, aquellos que están preparados, aquellos que están libres de pecado? Los dos textos indican que así pensó y dijo Jesús inicialmente. La mujer no aceptó esa norma cultural y social. No le gustaba vivir en un mundo donde la norma era la exclusión de las personas como ella y los de su clase. Transgredió el lenguaje homogéneo y dominante de esa cultura, tradición y religión e hizo que este hombre cambiara de opinión y de actitud. Generó conocimiento sentando las bases de una nueva posibilidad epistemológica: "De la boca de los pequeños y de los que todavía maman has establecido la alabanza frente a tus adversarios para hacer callar al enemigo y al vengativo". (Sal. 8:2)

También es interesante, en términos del contexto literario, que este texto se encuentra entre otros dos que mencionan el pan:

Mateo 14:13–21. Primera distribución de panes a los 5 000 hombres; 12 canastas sobrantes.
Mateo 15:21–28. Nuestra historia del conflicto sobre quién puede acceder a Jesús, al pan o a las migas.
Mateo 15:32–38. Segunda distribución de panes a los 4 000 hombres; siete canastas sobrantes.

Encontramos la correlación en Marcos al igual que en Mateo. Parece que la historia de la mujer sirofenicia, que discutió con Jesús acerca del acceso al pan o de obtener la sanación, resultó en la necesidad de volver a contar la primera historia de la multiplicación de las hogazas de pan y a darle otro final, afirmando que todas las personas tienen acceso a Jesús. Aquí, es conveniente recordar que tener acceso a Jesús es tener acceso a la comunidad, a un nuevo proyecto y al espacio político e ideo-teológico que va contra la corriente de lo que estaba establecido entonces y lo que está establecido ahora.

Todos tienen acceso a Jesús/la mesa/la comunión/la comunidad/el diálogo

> Ya no hay judío ni griego, no hay esclavo ni libre,
> no hay varón ni mujer; porque todos ustedes son
> uno en Cristo Jesús.
> **—Gálatas 3:28**

El acceso a Jesús, al pan o a las migas que caen de la mesa se relaciona con los encuentros e incompatibilidades entre personas de diferentes culturas con léxicos diferentes y distintas necesidades y deseos de aprender unos de otros. Por eso, nuestro texto hace tanto énfasis en la cultura y la geografía de los dos personajes y en sus necesidades: la mujer y su hija, sin relación ni participación (sin pan, mesa, salud, comunión, apoyo ni reconocimiento), y Jesús y sus discípulos más allegados (que, cabe mencionar, son hombres), atrapados por el etnocentrismo cultural que causa xenofobia y violencia. No obstante, estos hombres fueron bendecidos con la habilidad de escuchar, incluso en desacuerdo, para superar su supuesta superioridad y permanecer en el diálogo hasta el final. Parece que solo en un proceso dialógico puede aparecer la salud y la vida. Cabría, quizá, hacer una advertencia a la comunidad: la apertura a nuevas relaciones, a la escucha espiritual y vocacional, la solidaridad, el sentido de la igualdad y el intercambio son necesarios para transformar los desacuerdos en encuentros de amor y vida. Dichos encuentros evitan la enfermedad y la muerte y nos transforman. En 1 Corintios 11:28-32, Pablo condena la práctica de la cena en la comunidad corintia: comer sin examinarse uno mismo. Muchas personas actualmente están enfermas y débiles y algunas ya han muerto porque no han recibido el apoyo de la comunidad. De ahí se deriva el exhorto a examinarse uno mismo, para no condenarse a sí mismo.

Necesitamos "desaprender". "Dios ha elegido lo vil del mundo y lo menospreciado; lo que no es, para deshacer lo que es" (1 Cor. 1:27–28). Jesús, o la comunidad, desaprendieron algo para aprehender mucho más. Los encuentros entre culturas diferentes provocan esto cuando estamos verdaderamente abiertos y dispuestos a movernos hacia el desapego de nuestras verdades, tradiciones y certezas. De esta manera, podemos poner atención a la actitud fundamental de nuestra espiritualidad de liberación: escuchar y obedecer a Dios que da la vida y viene a nosotros en un mundo plural y diverso.

La mujer no pierde la motivación por el problema de no ser atendida. Es una víctima, pero no es pasiva. Tiene derechos, y su conocimiento de ellos le da fuerza (dinamo) para avanzar (enfrentar). Incluso desde su condición de "perro" (que ella misma se adjudica), ella afirma que no es un problema que le impida participar plenamente en la comunión.

Esta narrativa, en mi opinión, se une a otras al destacar la necesidad de que nuestra mentalidad, nuestras teologías, nuestras prácticas y nuestro cuidado pastoral sea anti-racista, anti-xenófobo y esté en contra de cualquier tipo de violencia. De la misma manera, nos llama a atender incondicionalmente a aquellos que necesitan ayuda y a poner atención a los conflictos que esto puede causar en la comunidad eclesiástica y en nuestra casa común, la *ecúmene,* y el planeta. ¿Buscamos el diálogo y permanecemos en el diálogo incluso cuando nos ofenden, nos descalifican y nos rebajan nuestra humanidad? ¿Cómo podemos convertir esto en una práctica que se extienda a los ambientes y contextos en los que vivimos?

Salir y encontrar a otras personas siempre es un desafío. Pero es nuestra decisión. ¿Estamos escuchando, como el sembrador de la parábola,[10] el llamado a sembrar, sin importar cuán difícil sea el terreno?

Que la Trinidad nos bendiga con el espíritu de indignación y resiliencia característico de nuestra espiritualidad.

10 Mateo 13:3–8; Marcos 4:3–8; Lucas 8:5–8.

MIÉRCOLES 7 DE SEPTIEMBRE

EL AMOR DE CRISTO EL VÍNCULO DE LA UNIDAD CRISTIANA Y EL TESTIMONIO COMÚN DE LAS IGLESIAS

Kenneth Mtata

[20] Entonces se acercó a él la madre de los hijos de Zebedeo con sus hijos, postrándose ante él y pidiéndole algo. [21] Él le dijo: "¿Qué deseas?" Ella le dijo: "Ordena que en tu reino estos dos hijos míos se sienten el uno a tu derecha y el otro a tu izquierda". [22] Entonces respondiendo Jesús dijo: "No saben lo que piden. ¿Pueden beber la copa que yo he de beber?" Ellos le dijeron: "Podemos". [23] Les dijo: "A la verdad, beberán de mi copa; pero el sentarse a mi derecha o a mi izquierda no es mío concederlo, sino que es para quienes lo ha preparado mi Padre". [24] Cuando los diez oyeron esto, se enojaron contra los dos hermanos. [25] Entonces Jesús los llamó y les dijo: "Saben que los gobernantes de los gentiles se enseñorean de ellos, y los que son grandes ejercen autoridad sobre ellos. [26] Entre ustedes no será así. Más bien, cualquiera que anhele ser grande entre ustedes será su servidor; [27] y el que anhele ser el primero entre ustedes, será su siervo. [28] De la misma manera, el Hijo del Hombre no vino para ser servido, sino para servir y para dar su vida en rescate por muchos".

—Mateo 20:20–28

La madre de los dos hijos de Zebedeo se acercó a Jesús en la postura más reverente, cercana a la postración (προσκυνοῦσα), para rogar que les concediera un favor a sus dos hijos. Aunque sus hijos son conocidos por el nombre de su padre, Zebedeo, ella usa su autoridad matriarcal para suplicar su exaltación, típica de aquellas culturas tradicionales donde el liderazgo explícito es patriarcal, pero el poder real lo determinan las mujeres fuera de la vista del público. De cualquier manera, ella busca para sus hijos lo que el Evangelio de Mateo presenta como objetivo final: "Más bien, busquen primeramente el reino de Dios y su justicia, y todas estas cosas les serán añadidas". (Mateo 6:33).

¿Qué conforma su comprensión del "reino"? Algunos estudiosos han preferido interpretar la referencia de Mateo al reino en el contexto de la "comunidad judeocristiana en el proceso de redefinir su propia identidad de oposición contra los judíos que se estaba consolidando bajo el liderazgo fariseo-escriba".[11] Otros ven todo el Evangelio de Mateo, en general, y la palabra *reino,* en particular, en el contexto más amplio del poder del imperio romano y su dominación.[12] Estos dos énfasis no son mutuamente excluyentes. Se sabe que los romanos, con su presencia concentrada en Antioquía, conformaron el contexto social de

11 A. B. Du Toit, "The Kingdom of God in the Gospel of Matthew," *Skrif en Kerk* 21, no. 3 (2000), 545. [Traducción libre al español.]

12 Boris Repschinsk, "Kingdoms of the Earth and the Kingdom of the Heavens: Matthew's Perspective on Political Power," (Reinos de la Tierra y el reino de los cielos: La perspectiva de Mateos sobre el poder político" en *The Composition, Theology, and Early Reception of Matthew's Gospel*, ed. Joseph Verheyden, Jens Schröter, y David C. Sim (Tübingen: Mohr Siebeck, 2022), 149 [Inglés].

las comunidades en el Evangelio de Mateo. Estos romanos eran los "gentiles" en los que se pensaría primeramente. Ejercieron un poder dominante sobre sus súbditos colonizados a través de una administración política flexible y representativa, pero también a través de su presencia militar y su dominación religiosa. Efectivamente, este aspecto los romanos estaban ejerciendo "poder sobre" (κατακυριεύουσιν) sus súbditos. Y como todas las personas colonizadas, los discípulos y sus comunidades se sentían atraídas e imitaban el exceso de poder que mostraban los opresores romanos. Por tanto, no es sorprendente que hayan buscado crear sus propios pequeños imperios, caracterizados por el "poder" dominante y las relaciones tiránicas. En este sentido, la madre de los hijos de Zebedeo busca puestos principales para sus hijos. Al hacerlo, también espera garantizarse ella misma un lugar especial en el reino.

En Mateo 20, en cambio, Jesús está ofreciendo una nueva versión del poder como poder a través del servicio abnegado y humilde (vv. 26–27). En esta concepción es como mejor se entiende el reino de Dios: donde la grandeza se demuestra siendo servidor (διάκονος) e incluso esclavo (δοῦλος), donde el servicio prevalece hasta la muerte. En el contexto literario inmediato del pasaje de hoy, Jesús predice su muerte (vv. 17-19) y sana a los dos hombres ciegos (quizá haciendo contraste con los dos hijos de Zebedeo) mientras cuando pasa por Jericó (vv. 29-34). La muerte de Jesús es lo que abre los ojos a la grandeza verdadera. Jesús no solo es el maestro sino el ejemplo máximo de la *diaconía*, o el servicio humilde.

¿Qué significa esto para nosotros?

"Cuando los diez oyeron esto, se enojaron contra los dos hermanos". (v. 24). Mary Jane Gorman dice, "Podemos identificarnos con la ira de los otros diez discípulos: Si nos hemos resistido virtuosamente a pedir sentarnos junto al invitado de honor, podríamos tener resentimiento hacia otra persona que sí lo haya hecho"[13] De la misma manera que esta acción de búsqueda egoísta del poder amenazó la unidad de los discípulos, también sufre la unidad de la iglesia bajo el peso del poder dominante, controlador y privilegiado porque este, a su vez, genera reacciones de ira, celos y desconfianza.

Como en el contexto del Imperio Romano, el mundo hoy parece estar agobiado por formas de poder militaristas, excluyentes e idólatras. Esta expresión de poder opresor puede perpetrarse a través de alianzas patriarcales y matriarcales engañosas (como una madre que prepara un puesto especial para sus hijos), ideologías absolutistas de la derecha o la izquierda política ("el uno a tu derecha y el otro a tu izquierda"), o identidades nepotistas basadas en la raza o la etnicidad (hijos de Zebedeo), todos bajo la apariencia de religiosidad y devoción (en busca del reino de Dios).

La unidad de la iglesia puede sostenerse y revitalizarse, dice Jesús, a través del cambio de estas concepciones de poder, remplazándolas con el poder del servicio (*diaconía*). Este servicio es verdaderamente unificador si no quita el poder o remplaza la voluntad de quienes lo reciben. La *diaconía* que favorece la unidad de la iglesia se pone en práctica con amor, amor sacrificial. Este amor debe superar el amor maternal por dos hijos. Es el amor con el que Dios amó a toda la humanidad. Este es el amor que trasciende las alianzas

13 Mary Jane Gorman, *Watching the Disciples: Learning from Their Mistakes*, (Nashville, TN: Abingdon Press, 2008), https://books.google.co.za/books?id=-ax0qIW55nkC&pg.

patriarcales y matriarcales pero que construye nuevas alianzas de amor entre hermanos y hermanas de la familia de Dios. Este amor expande el círculo para incluir a aquellos que normalmente serían descalificados. Este amor rompe las barreras de la raza, la intolerancia étnica y el orgullo. Es un amor que nos hace humildes sin humillarnos.

En humildad, este amor se expresa en el servicio abnegado de un esclavo, el *duolos*. El amor que acoge este tipo de servicio no se basa en sentimientos eróticos ni pasionales. No es solamente filial ni se basa en la amistad. No se basa necesariamente en el amor de los padres por sus hijos o el amor de parientes y conocidos. Su fuente debe ser el amor ágape, el amor de todos los que fueron creados a imagen y semejanza de Dios. Este es el amor que Dios compartió con nosotros en Jesucristo. Es el amor que puede quitar el veneno de las formas opresoras de poder en la iglesia y en el mundo.

La iglesia, impulsada por este amor, es un testigo poderoso en el mundo porque ofrece una manera alternativa de expresar el poder. El ejercicio del poder por parte de la iglesia no puede reflejar el ejercicio del poder del mundo. Debe ser la sal y la luz del mundo. La iglesia contribuye a la transformación de los esquemas sesgados de poder en el mundo a través del testimonio de sus miembros, que viven en la sociedad como representantes del reino venidero de Dios. A través de sus vidas ejemplares y de sus palabras, en sus familias, en sus comunidades, en la iglesia y en la esfera pública, prevalecerán contra las puertas de Hades.

La iglesia también es testigo del mundo cuando toma posiciones absolutas que a veces no son populares o seguras. "Pero sea su hablar, 'sí', 'sí', y 'no', ' no'. Porque lo que va más allá de esto, procede del mal". (Mateo 5:37). El testimonio valiente y abnegado de la iglesia tiene como fin resistir, socavar y, finalmente, extirpar todos los sistemas que generan relaciones de poder injustas y desiguales en el mundo y en la iglesia. Las iglesias fieles deben ser capaces de decir: ¡entre nosotros no debe ser así! Las iglesias deben decirlo a nivel local, regional, nacional y global. La iglesia debe decir "no" al militarismo creciente, a los mercados no productivos, al materialismo, al monoculturalismo, a la manipulación, a la desinformación, a la malicia, a la justicia popular y al monopolio expansivo sobre el público y la gente común. Por la misma veta, la iglesia debe gritar un "sí" empático. Debe decir sí a la misericordia y a la compasión, a las relaciones significativas, a la cooperación multilateral de las naciones, a las soluciones mediadas a los conflictos, a la moderación de las posturas y a la reciprocidad. ¡Esta es la reorganización del poder a la que Jesús nos llama!

AUTORES COLABORADORES

La Revda. Dra. **Hyunju Bae** fue profesora en la Universidad Presbiteriana de Busan en la República de Corea, y ministra ordenada en la Iglesia Presbiteriana de Corea. Prestó sus servicios a los comités ejecutivo y central del Consejo Mundial de Iglesias en el periodo entre Busan y Karlsruhe. Es copresidenta del Movimiento Ambiental Cristiano de Corea, Solidaridad para la Integridad de la Creación.

Archimandrita Prof. Dr. **Jack Khalil** del Patriarcado Griego Ortodoxo de Antioquia y de todo Oriente. Decano del Instituto de Teología San Juan de Damasco de la Universidad de Balamand y profesor de estudios del Nuevo Testamento. Tiene un doctorado de la Universidad Aristóteles de Tesalónica y estudió por tres años como profesor visitante en la Universidad de Tubinga, Alemania. Es miembro del Comité Central y de la Comisión de Fe y Constitución del CMI.

El Dr. **Krzysztof Mielcarek** es teólogo, académico biblista y profesor adjunto de la Facultad de Teología de la Universidad Católica Juan Pablo II en Lublin, Polonia. Es uno de los editores y traductores de la Biblia Ecuménica Polaca (2007). Ha sido comisionado católico romano de la Comisión de Fe y Constitución del Consejo Mundial de Iglesias desde 2014.

Rev. Dr. **Kenneth Mtata** es un teólogo zimbabuense y secretario general del Consejo de Iglesias de Zimbabue. Ha trabajado en la hermenéutica, la participación pública de las iglesias y la interfase de la transformación religiosa y social. Su doctorado en la Universidad de KwaZulu-Natal fue en el Espacio y el Lugar en el Evangelio de Juan.

La Dra. **Diana Tsaghikyan** es profesora adjunta en la Facultad de Teología de la Yerevan State University, y jefa del programa de estudios de grado. También es miembro del comité de tesis de doctorado en el Seminario Teológico de Geforkian (Universidad), Santa Sede de la Santa Etchmiadzin. La Dra. Tsaghikyan se unió al CMI en 2019 como representante de la Iglesia Apostólica Armenia (Santa Sede de la Santa Etchmiadzin) y miembro del Comité Central. Recibió su doctorado y su maestría en teología de la Universidad de Edimburgo, su maestría en Estudios Religiosos del Seminario Teológico Bautista Central en Kansas, USA, y su licenciatura de la Universidad Estatal de Lenguas y Ciencias Sociales de Ereván. Su investigación principal se enfoca en estudios de patrística y doctrina cristiana. Está especialmente interesada en la literatura teológica de los padres de la iglesia armenia. Sus otros intereses de investigación incluyen estudios ecuménicos y asuntos contemporáneos en la teología.

El Dr. **Paulo Ueti** es brasileño de madre japonesa y padre italiano. Es estudiante de teologías latinoamericanas, de estudios bíblicos contextuales y del canon del nuevo testamento y su relación con la historia de la iglesia, las teologías imperialistas, la espiritualidad, el género, la justicia climática y la eclesiología. Es miembro del Centro Ecuménico de Estudios Bíblicos (CEBI, por sus siglas en Portugués) de la Iglesia Episcopal Anglicana de Brasil y trabaja en Londres en la Oficina de la Comunión Anglicana con la Alianza Anglicana (Desarrollo, Asistencia y Defensa) y el Departamento de Educación Teológica.